EASY PIANO

JOSH GROBAN
ILLUMINATIONS

T0086574

Our thanks to David Romano, Josh Groban's Vocal Coach and
Music Supervisor, for his help in the preparation of this songbook.

ISBN 978-1-4584-1320-8

Hal•Leonard®
CORPORATION

7777 W. BLUEMOUND RD. P.O. BOX 13819 MILWAUKEE, WI 53213

Visit Hal Leonard Online at
www.halleonard.com

CONTENTS

4 THE WANDERING KIND (PRELUDE)

12 BELLS OF NEW YORK CITY

21 GALILEO (SOMEONE LIKE YOU)

29 L'ORA DELL'ADDIO

32 HIDDEN AWAY

38 AU JARDIN DES SANS-POURQUOI (THE GARDEN WITHOUT "WHYS")

43 HIGHER WINDOW

53 IF I WALK AWAY

62 LOVE ONLY KNOWS

70 VOCÊ EXISTE EM MIM

75 WAR AT HOME

81 LONDON HYMN

84 STRAIGHT TO YOU

THE WANDERING KIND
(Prelude)

By JOSH GROBAN

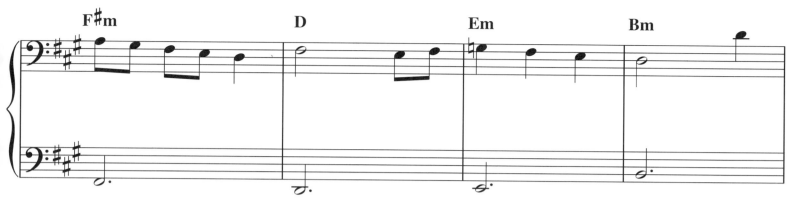

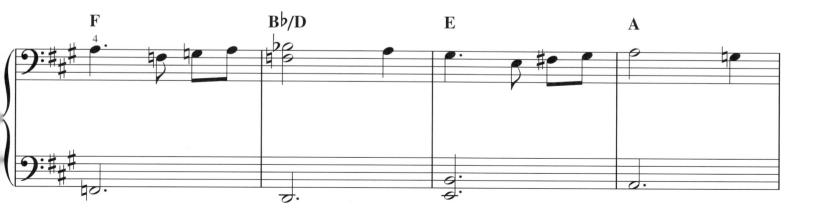

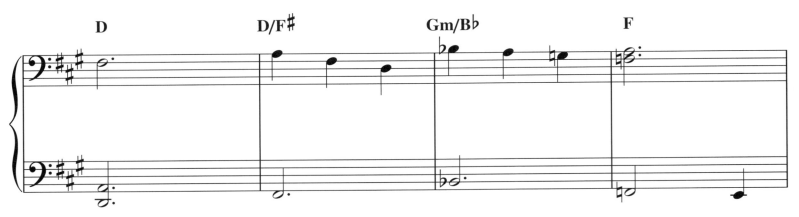

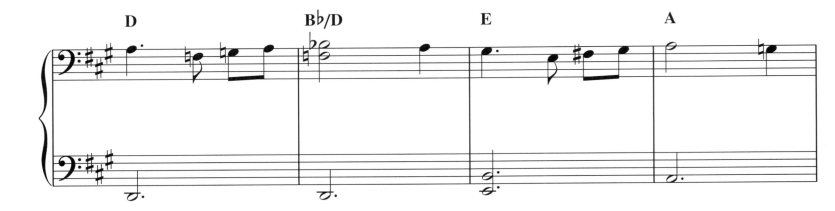

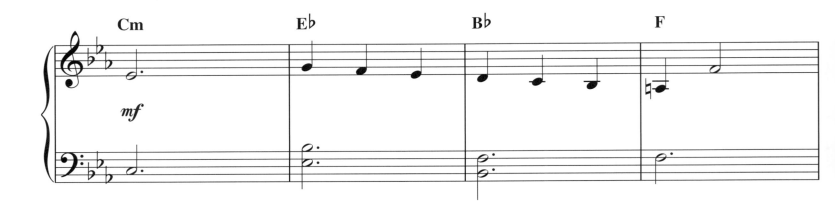

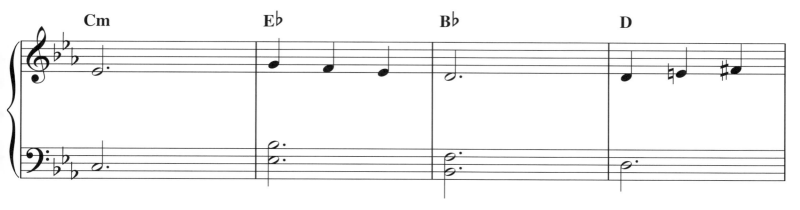

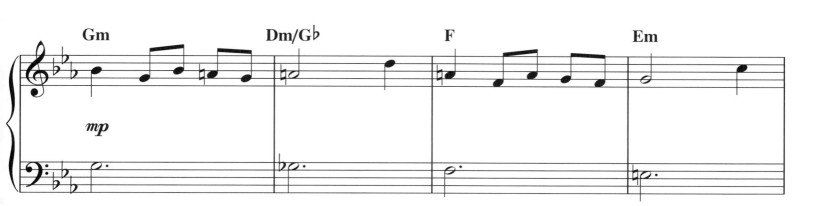

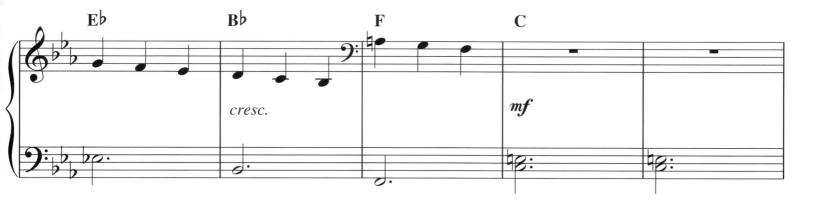

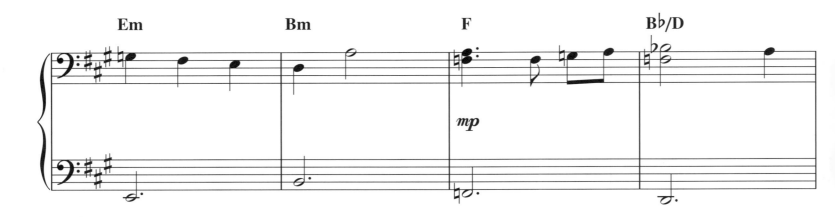

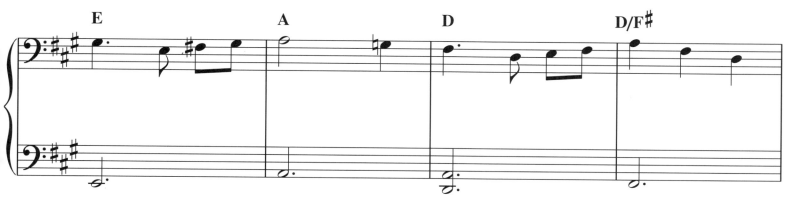

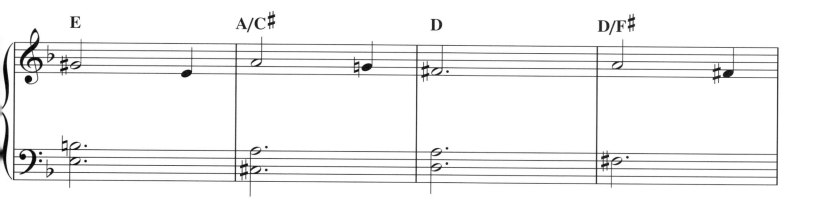

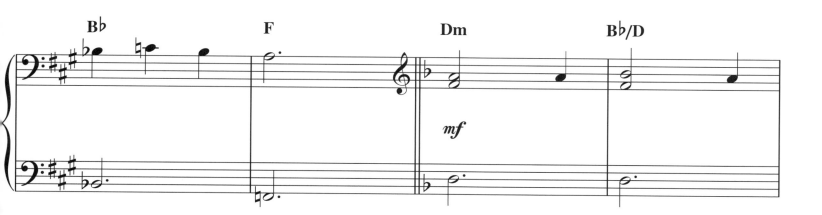

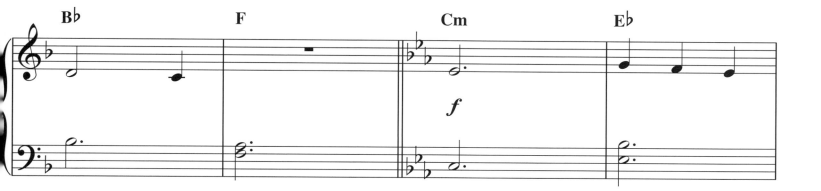

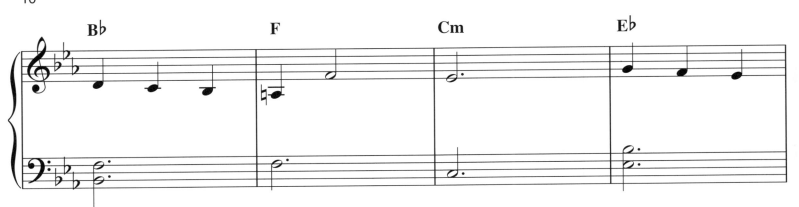

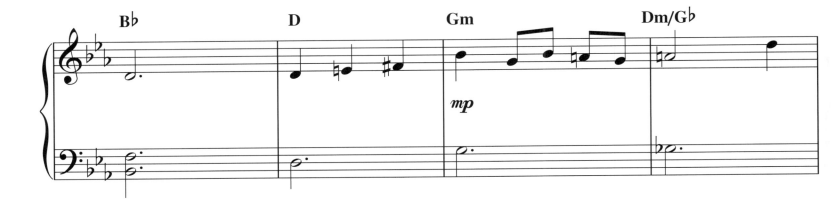

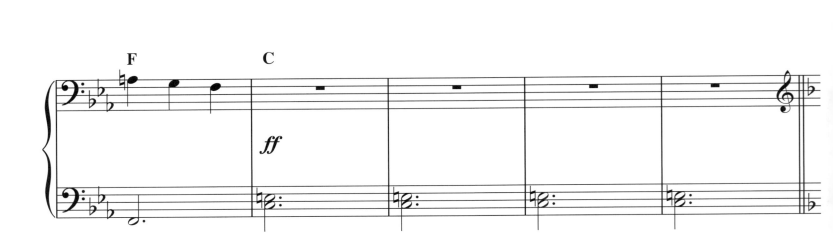

11

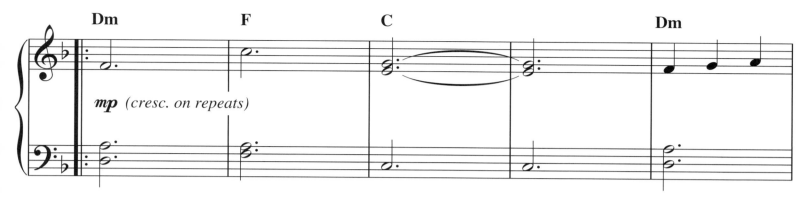

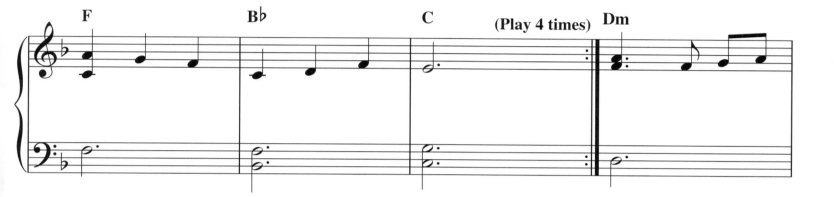

BELLS OF NEW YORK CITY

Words and Music by JOSH GROBAN
and DAN WILSON

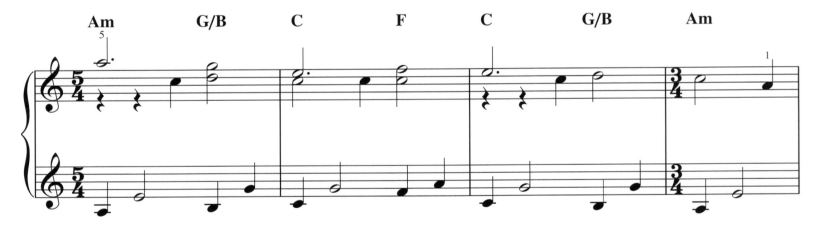

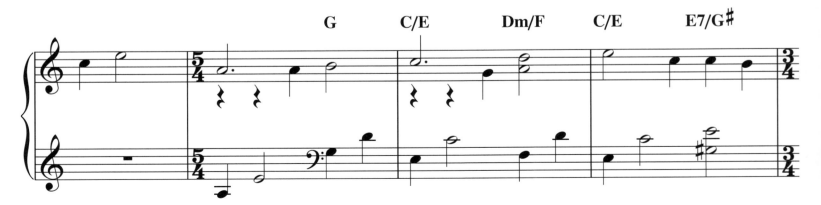

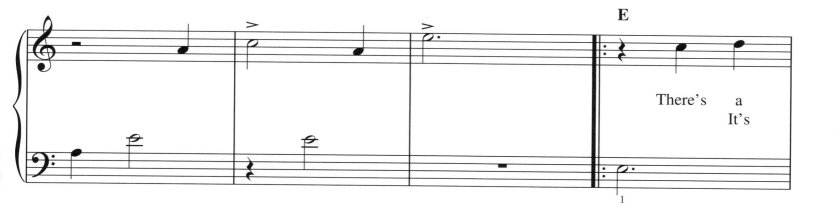

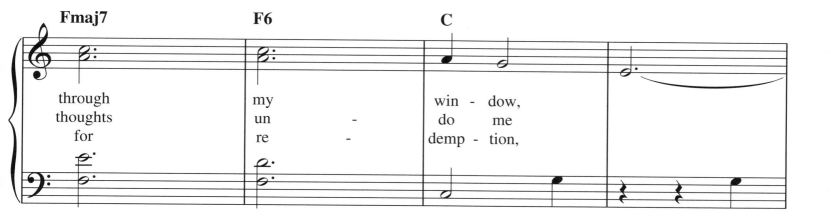

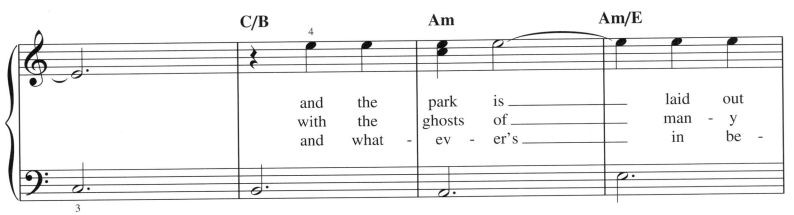

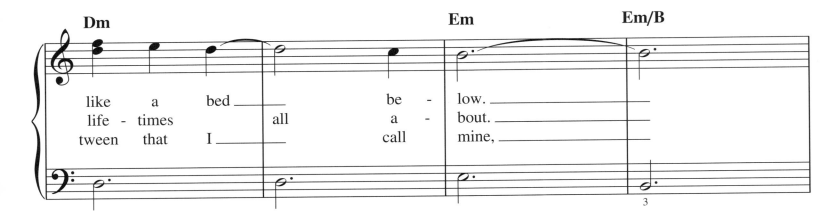

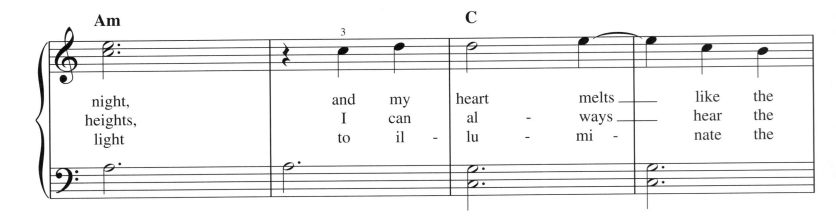

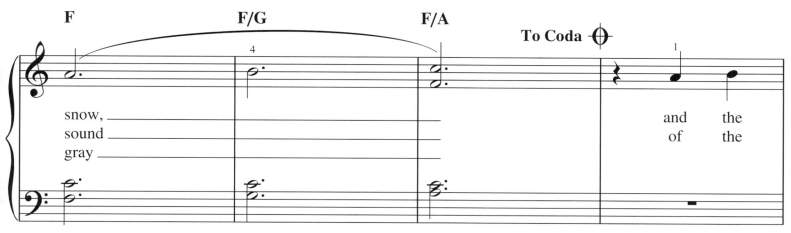

F   F/G   F/A   To Coda

snow, _____
sound _____ and   the
gray _____ of   the

Am   C/E   F   G

bells   of ___ New   York   Cit - y ___ tell   me
bells   of ___ New   York   Cit - y ___ sing - ing

Am9

not   to   go.
all   a - round.

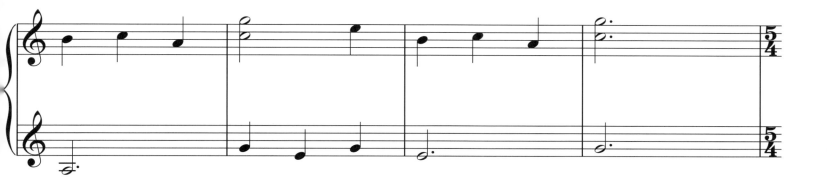

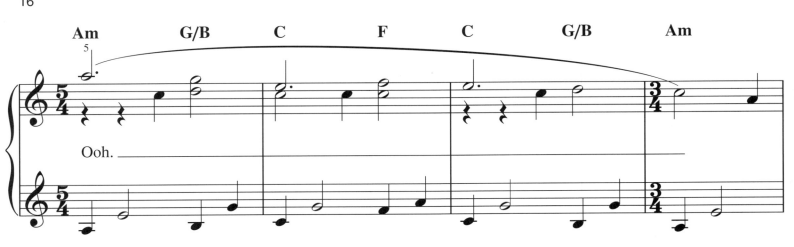

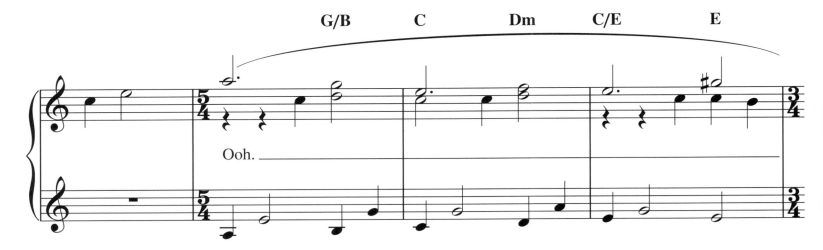

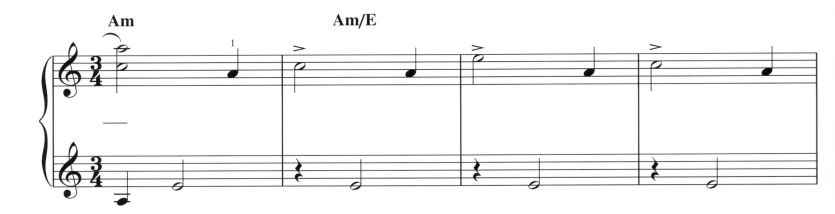

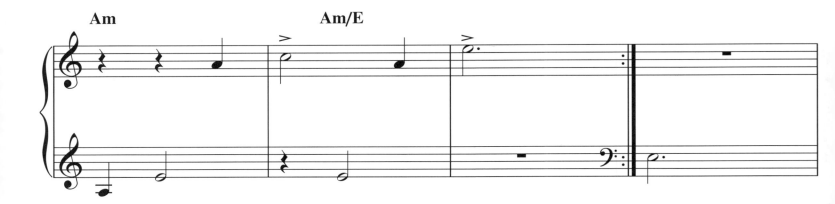

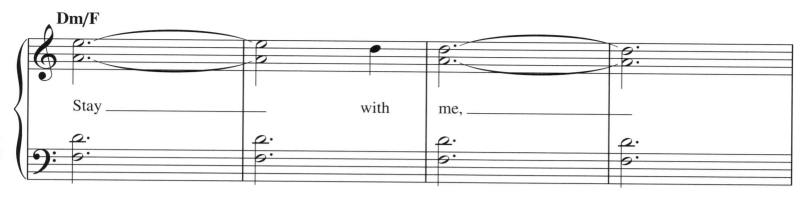

Stay _____ with me, _____

stay _____ with me, a

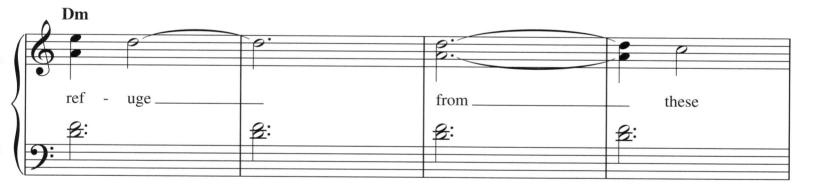

ref - uge _____ from _____ these

bro - ken dreams. _____

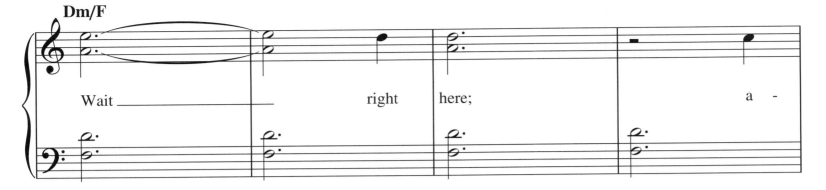

CODA

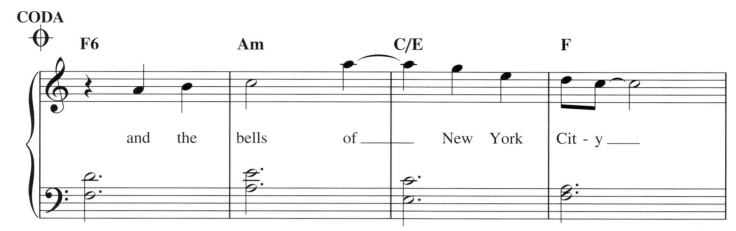

and the bells of _____ New York Cit - y _____

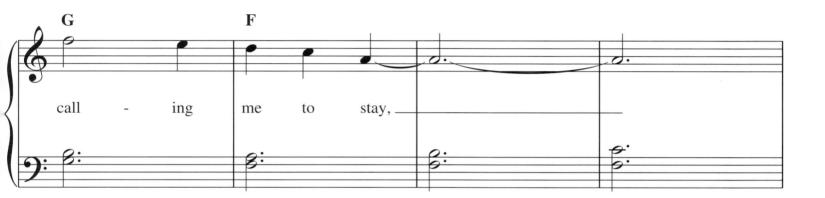

call - ing me to stay, _____

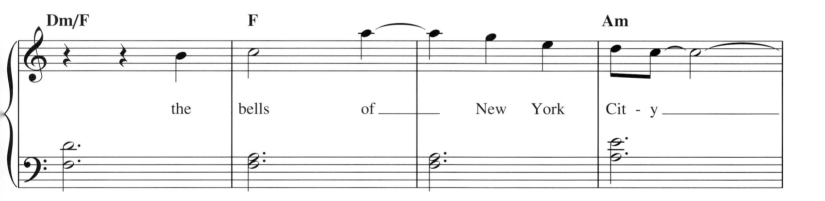

the bells of _____ New York Cit - y _____

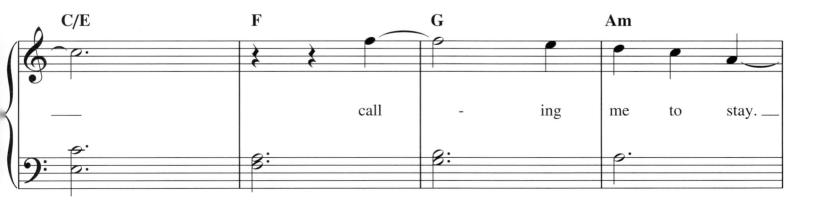

_____ call - ing me to stay. _____

20

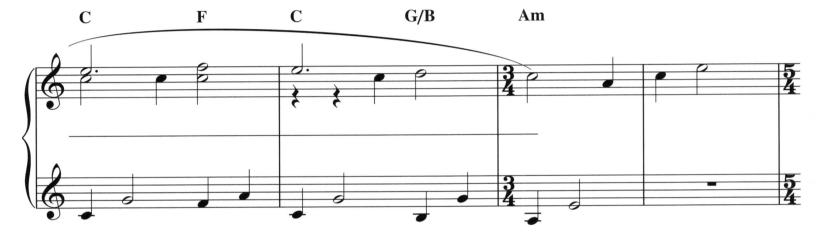

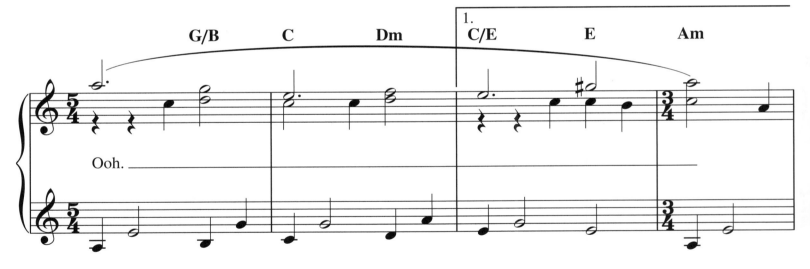

GALILEO
(Someone Like You)

Words and Music by DECLAN O'ROURKE
and SEAMUS COTTER

Moderately, with freedom

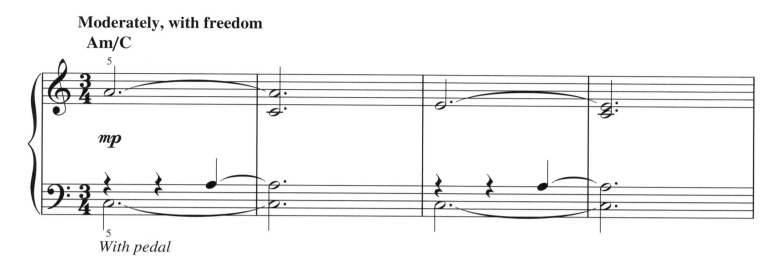

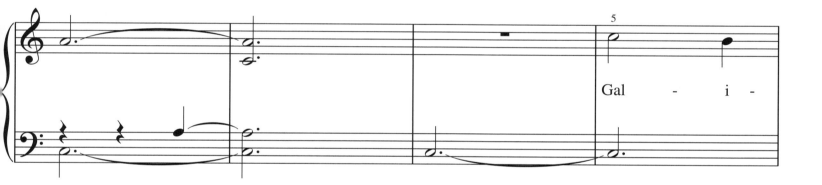

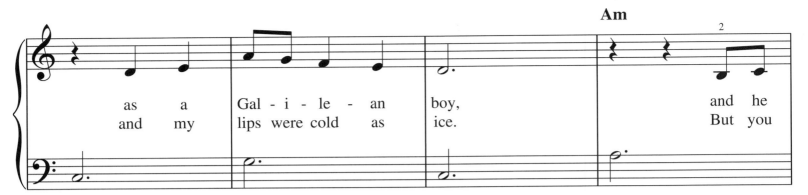

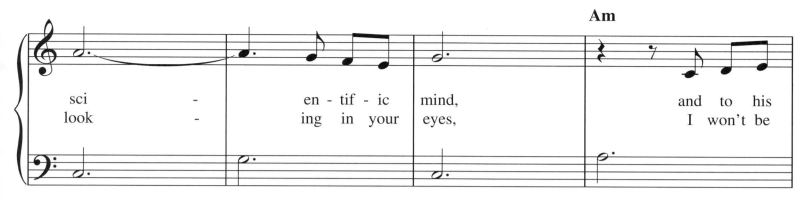

sci - en - tif - ic mind, and to his
look - ing in your eyes, I won't be

blind and dy - ing days, he looked up
blind, and I won't cry. I'll look up

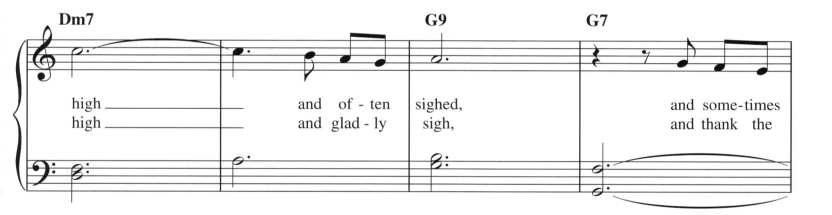

high and of - ten sighed, and some-times
high and glad - ly sigh, and thank the

cried, "Who puts the rain - bow in the
Guy who puts the rain - bow in the

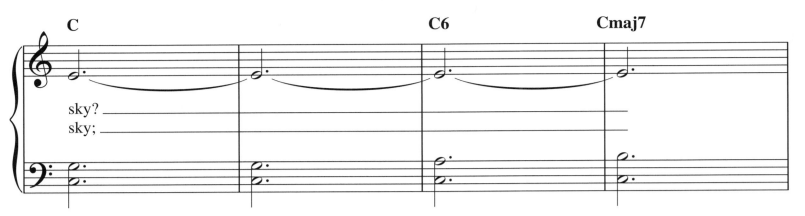

sky? _____
sky; _____

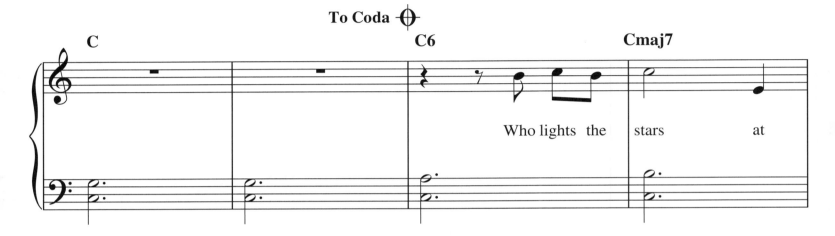

To Coda ⊕

Who lights the stars at

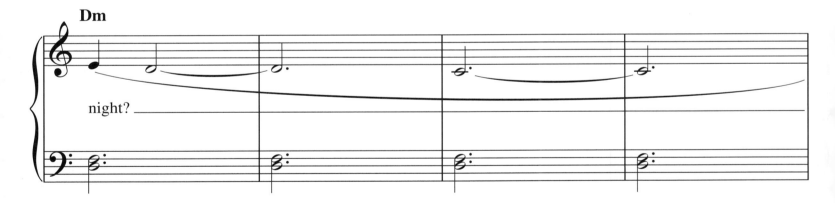

night? _____

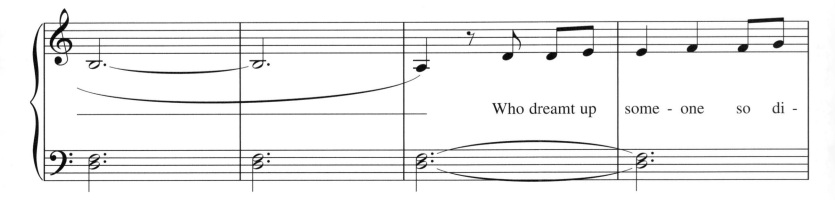

Who dreamt up some-one so di-

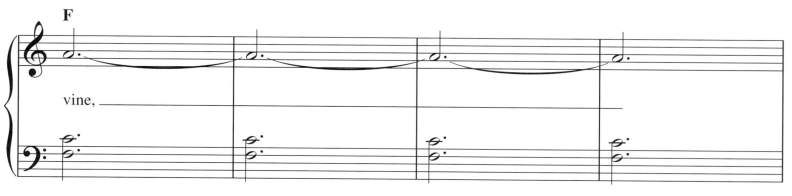

vine, _____

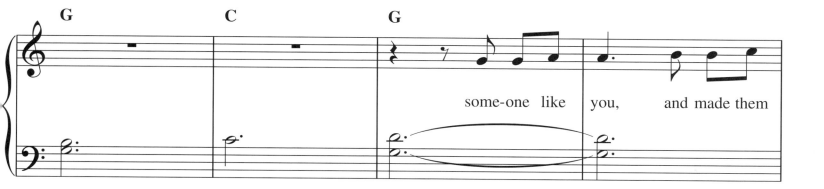

some-one   like   you,   and made them

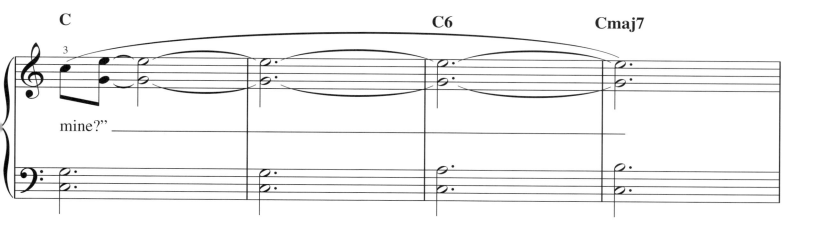

mine?" _____

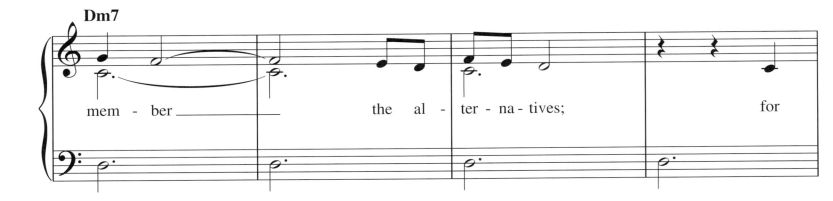

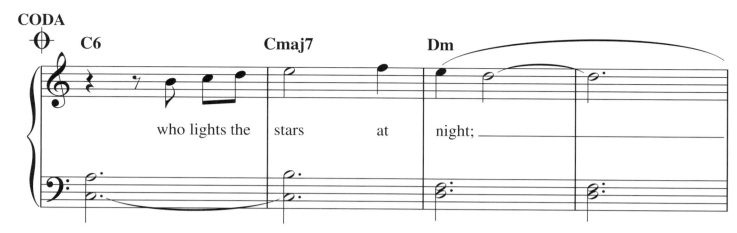

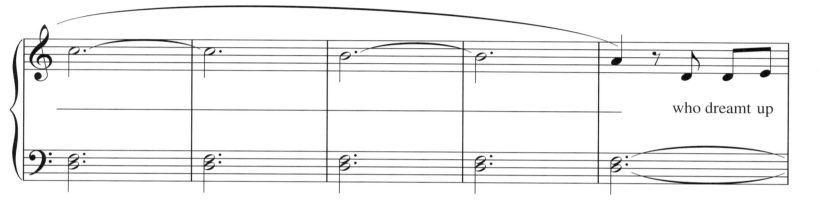

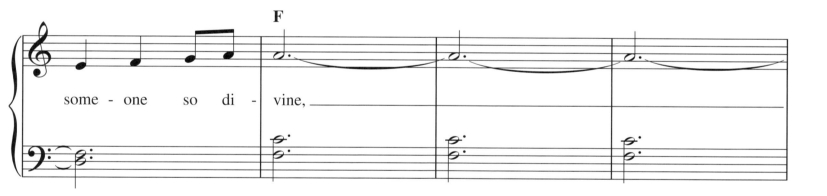

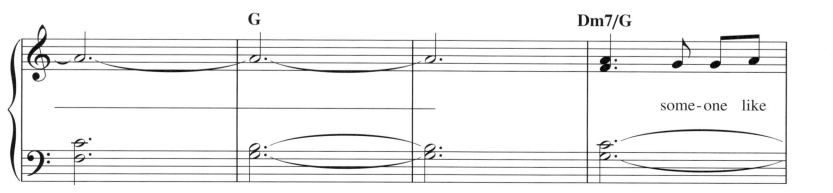

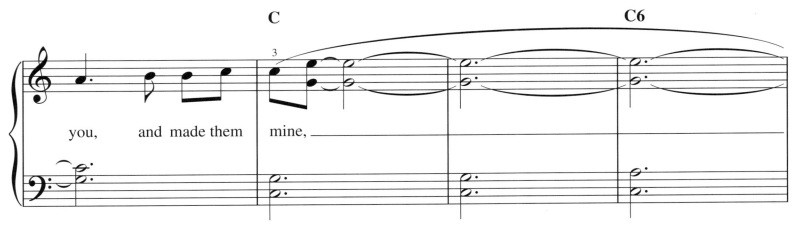

C **C6**

you, and made them mine, _____

Cmaj7 **C** **C6**

_____ some-one like

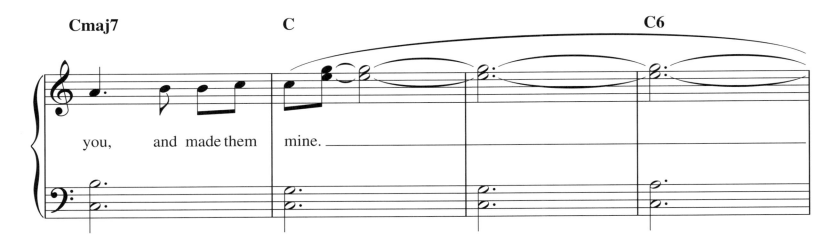

Cmaj7 **C** **C6**

you, and made them mine. _____

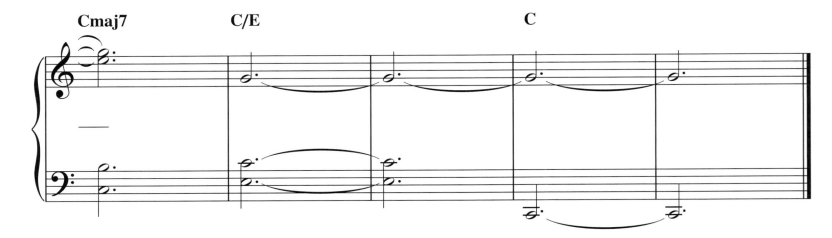

Cmaj7 **C/E** **C**

L'ORA DELL'ADDIO

Words and Music by JOSH GROBAN,
WALTER AFANASIEFF and MARCO MARINANGELI

Credi - di - mi   fa più ma - le den - tro   il do - ver an - dar - se -

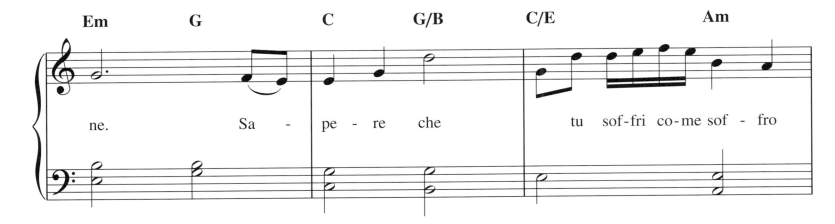

ne.   Sa - pe - re che   tu sof-fri co - me sof - fro

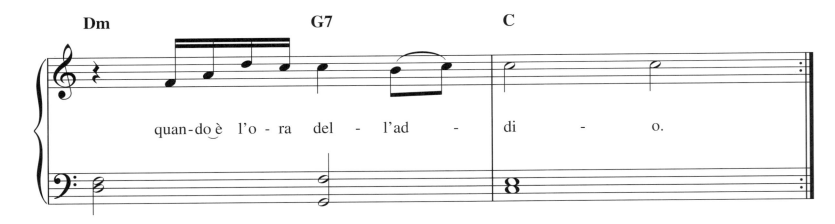

quan-do è l'o - ra del - l'ad - di - o.

Com' - è dif - fi - ci - le ig-no - ra - re le me-mo-rie di u-na vi - ta

4

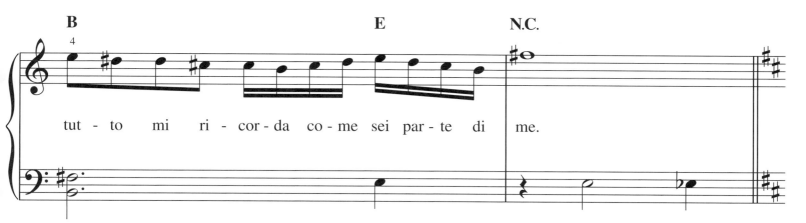

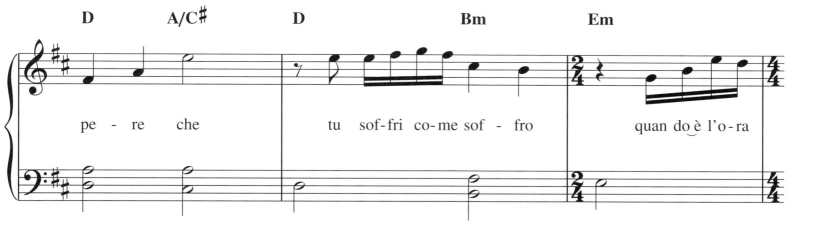

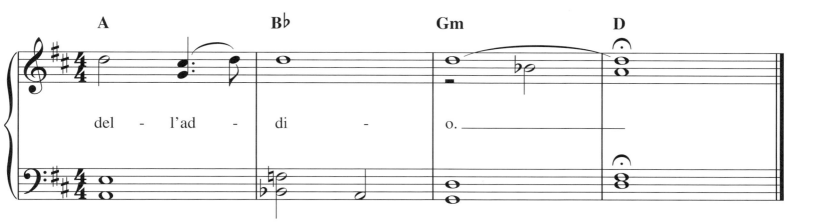

HIDDEN AWAY

Words and Music by JOSH GROBAN
and DAN WILSON

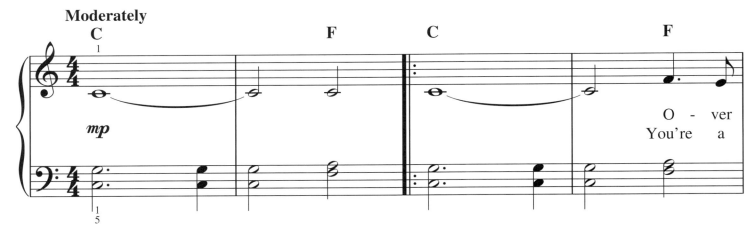

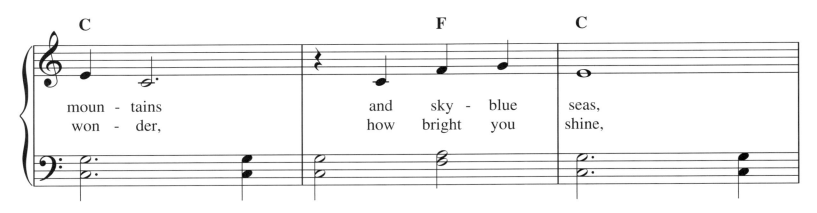

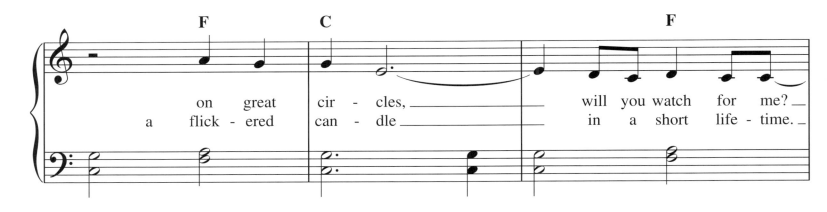

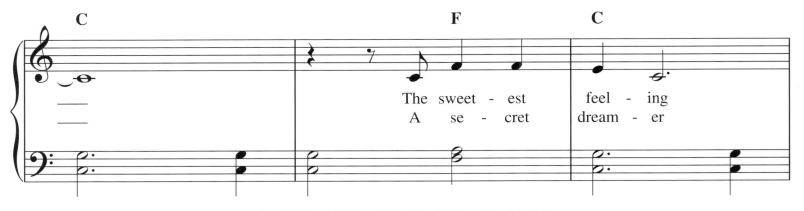

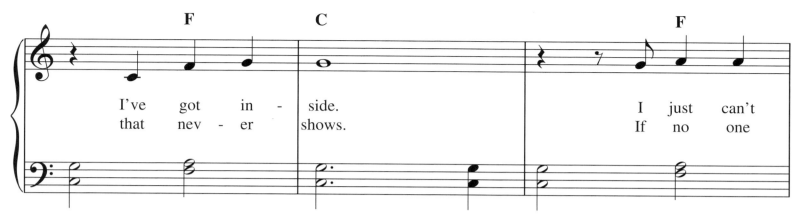

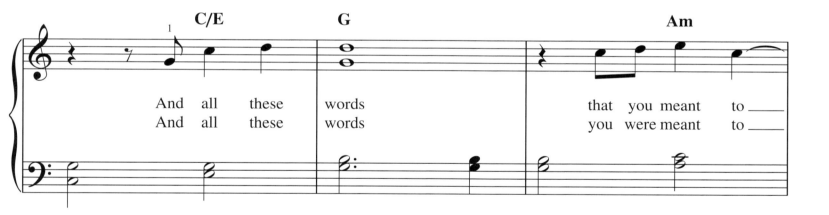

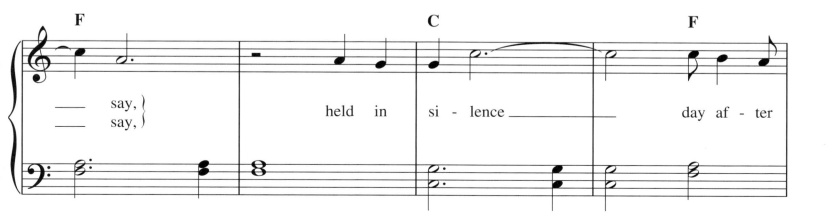

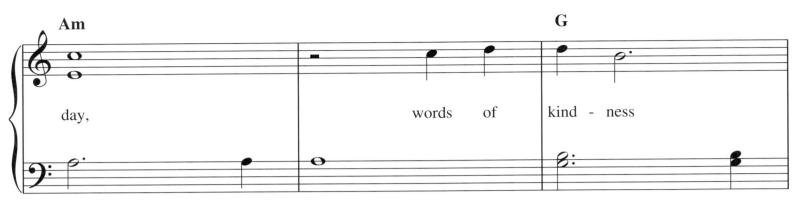

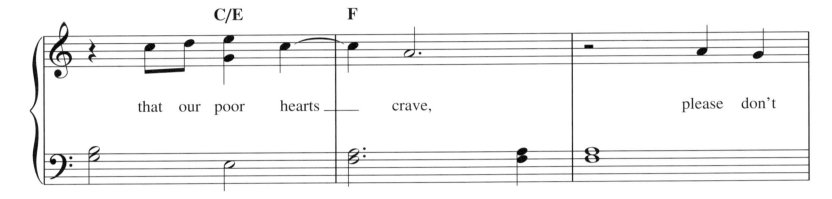

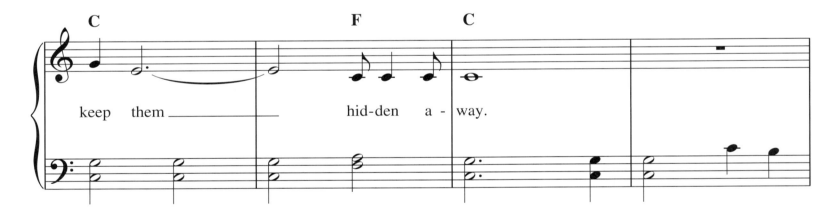

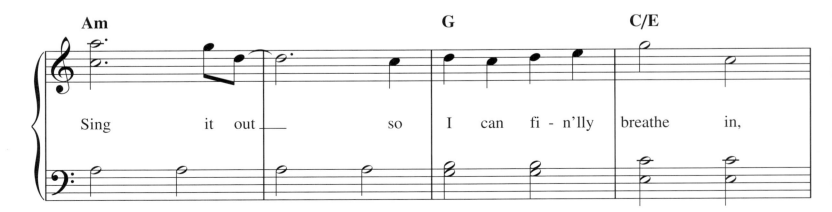

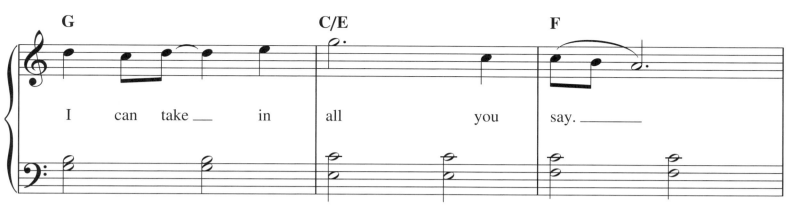

I can take ___ in all you say. ___

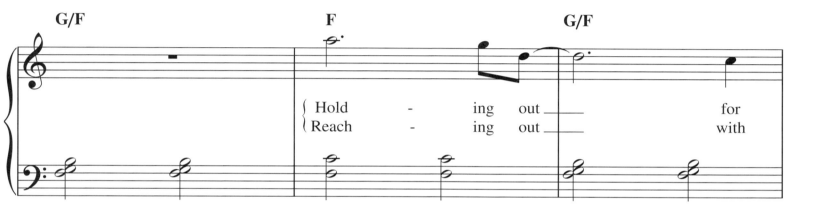

{ Hold - ing out ___ for
{ Reach - ing out ___ with

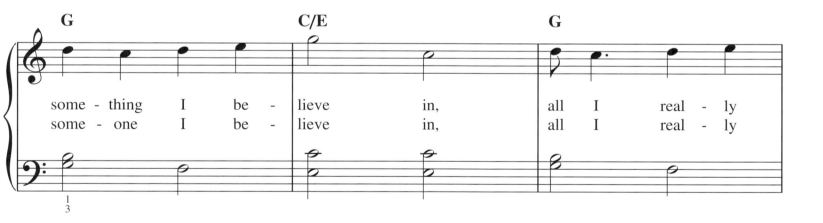

some - thing I be - lieve in, all I real - ly
some - one I be - lieve in, all I real - ly

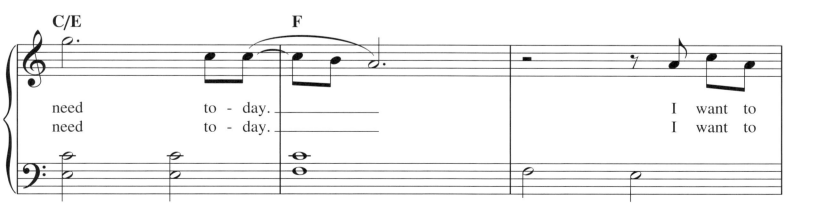

need to - day. ___ I want to
need to - day. ___ I want to

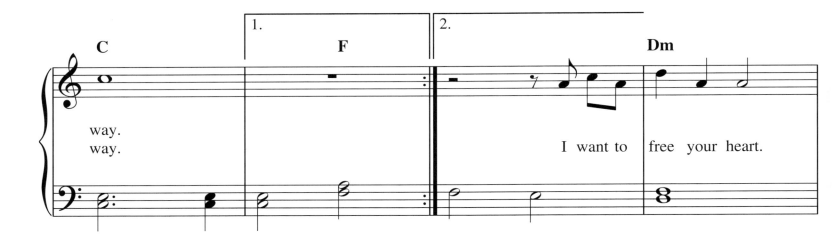

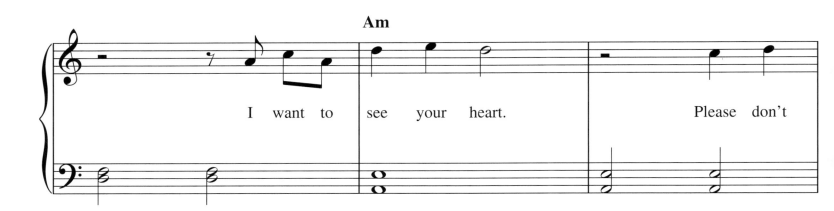

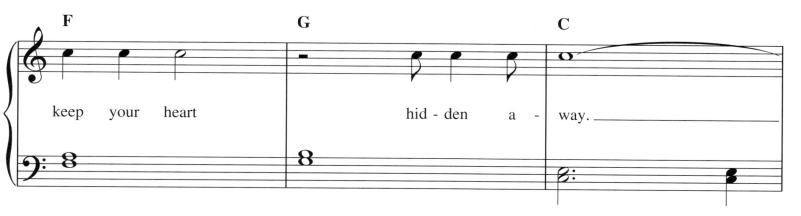

keep your heart   hid - den a - way. _____

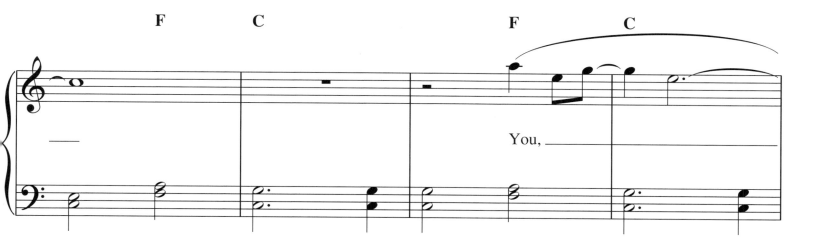

You, _____

you. _____   You, _____

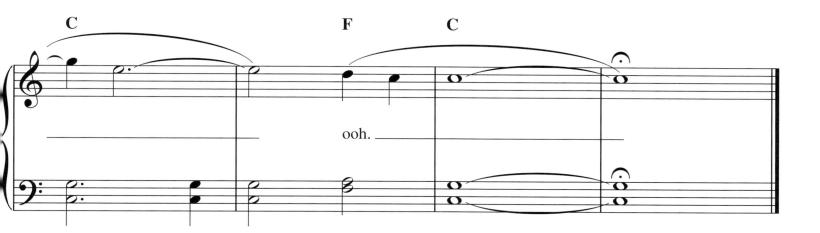

ooh. _____

AU JARDIN DES SANS-POURQUOI
(The Garden Without "Whys")

Words and Music by JOSH GROBAN,
KATE McGARRIGLE and RUFUS WAINWRIGHT

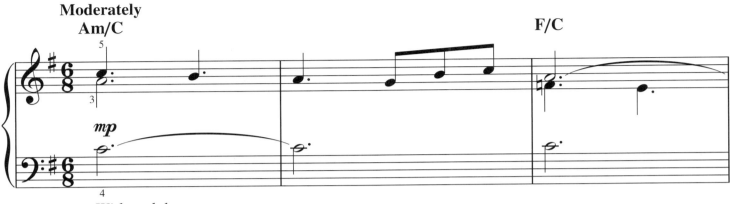

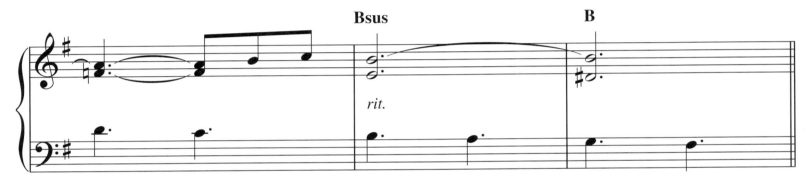

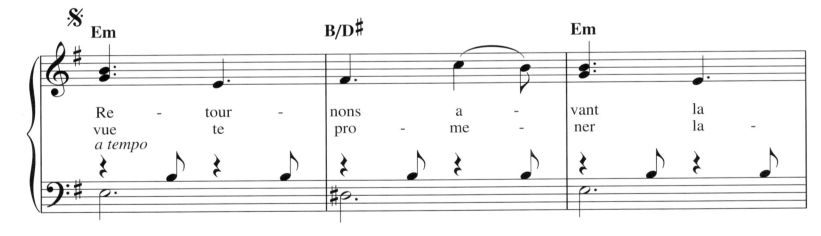

Re - tour - nons a - vant la
vue te pro - me - ner la

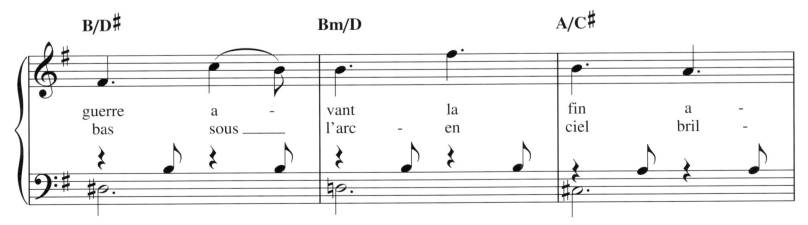

guerre a - vant la fin a -
bas sous ___ l'arc - en ciel a bril -

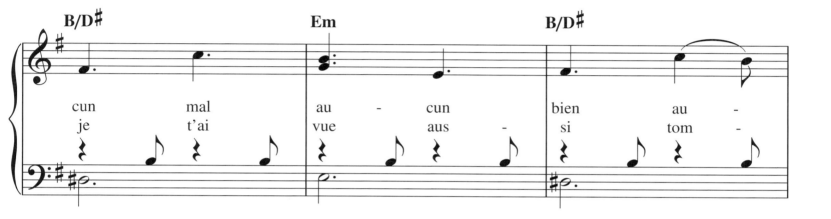

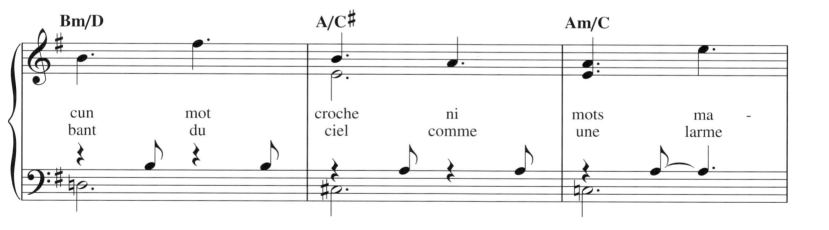

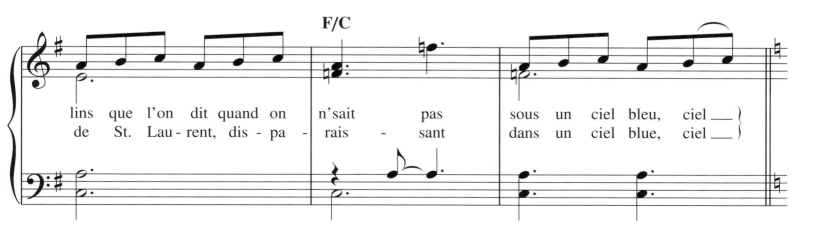

40

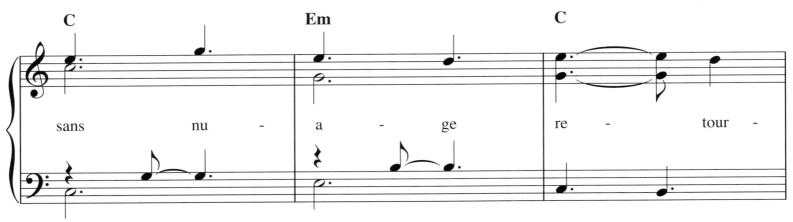

sans nu - a - ge re - tour -

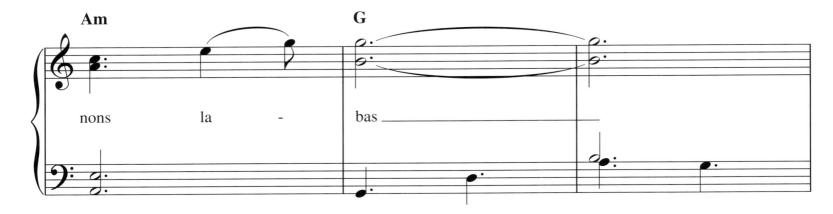

nons la - bas

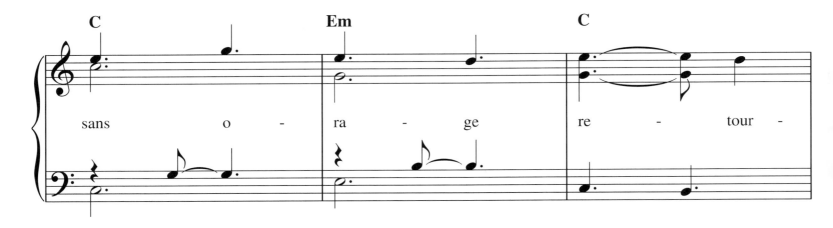

sans o - ra - ge re - tour -

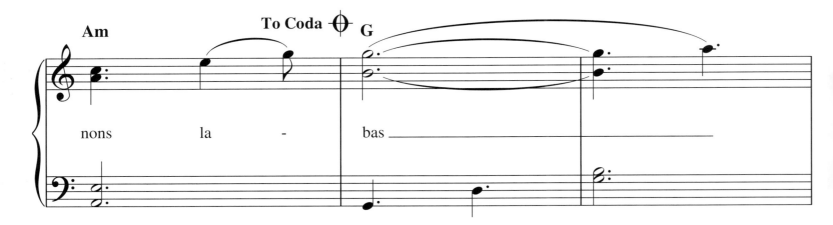

nons la - bas

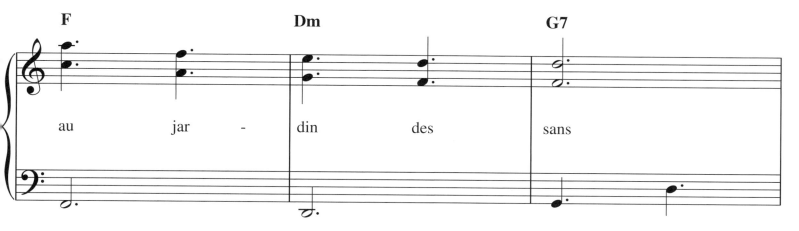

au   jar -   din   des   sans

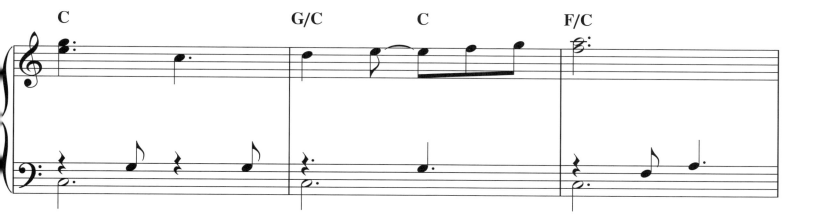

pour -   quoi.

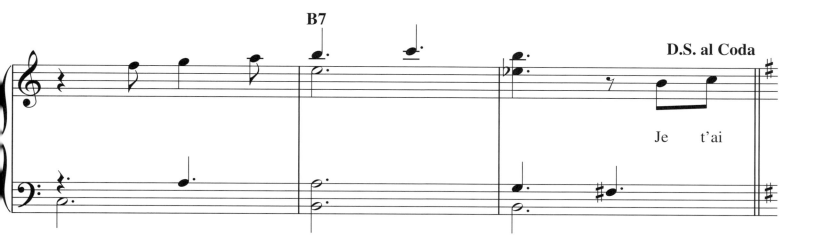

Je   t'ai

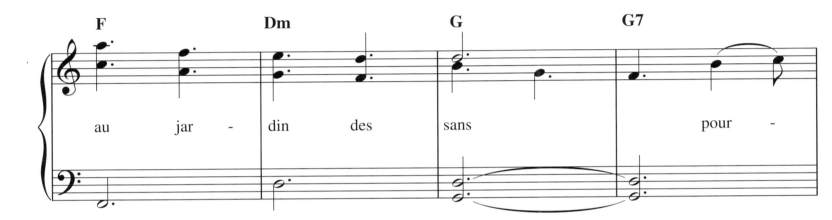

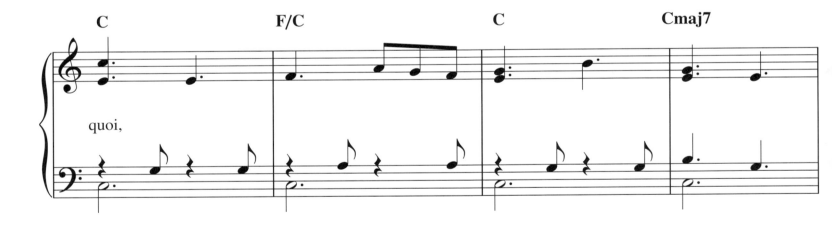

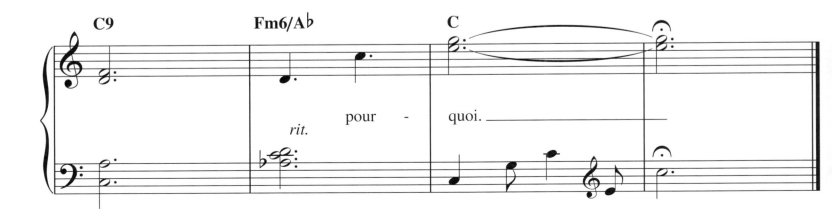

HIGHER WINDOW

Words and Music by JOSH GROBAN,
DAN WILSON and THOMAS SALTER

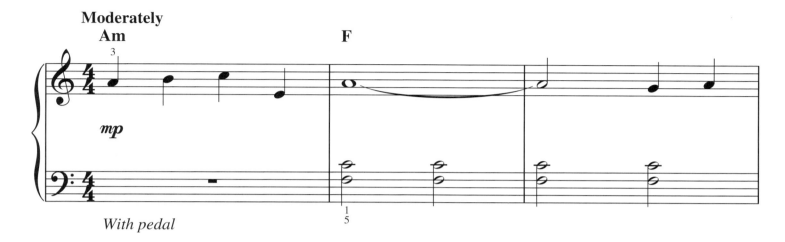

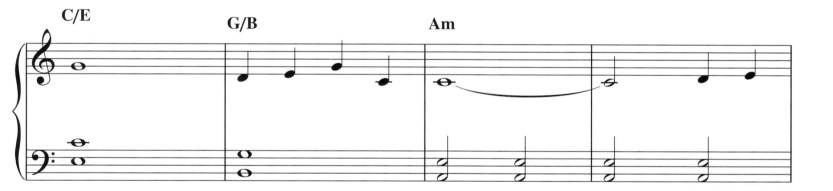

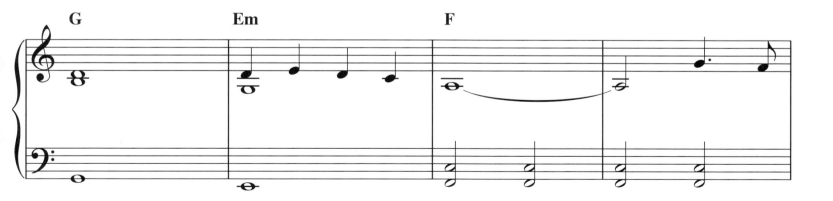

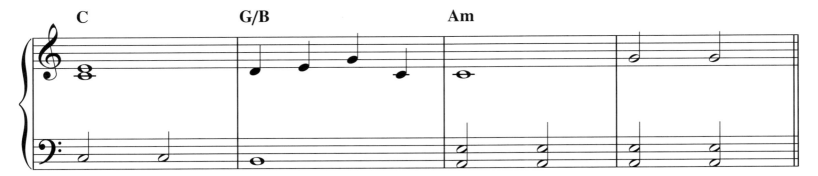

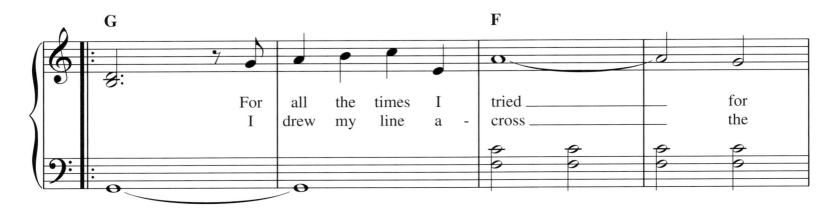

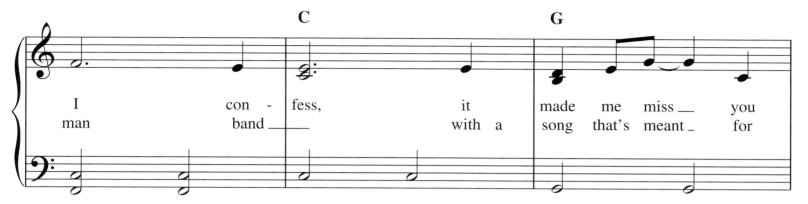

C   G

I   con - fess,   it   made me miss __ you

man   band ___   with a   song that's meant _ for

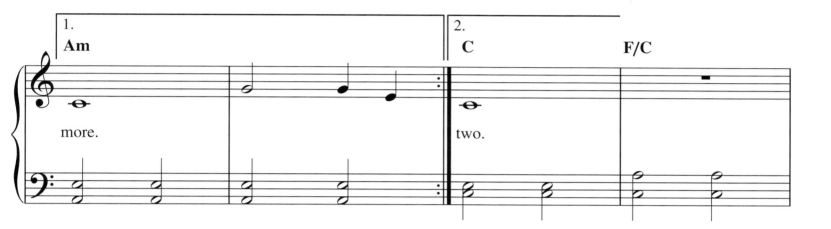

1.
Am   2.
                               C   F/C

more.   two.

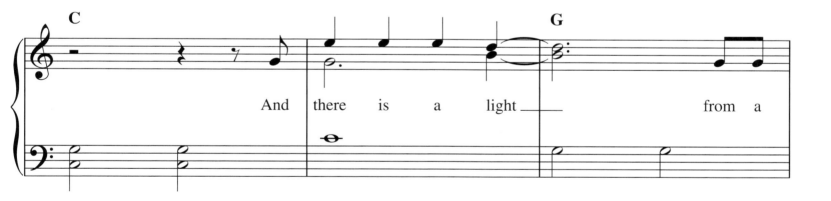

C   G

And there is a light ___   from a

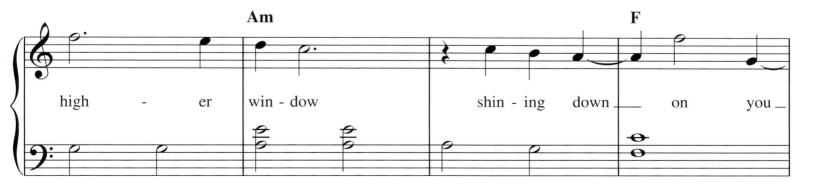

                 Am   F

high - er win - dow   shin - ing down __ on you __

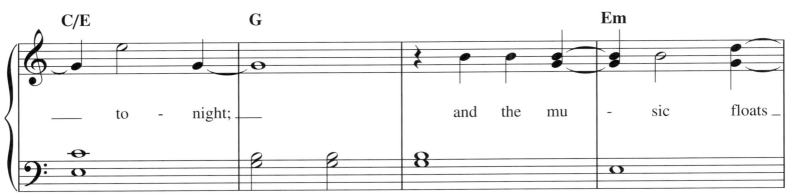

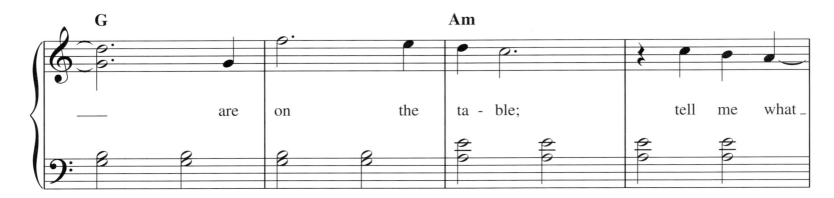

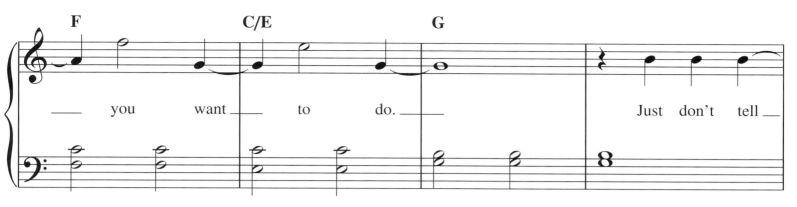

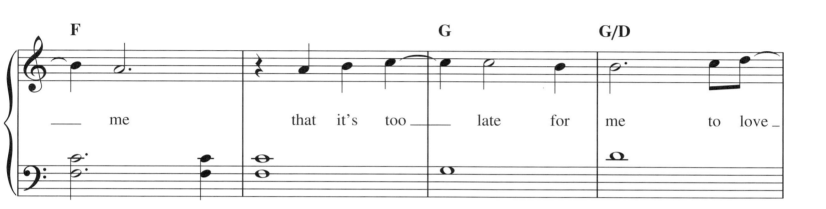

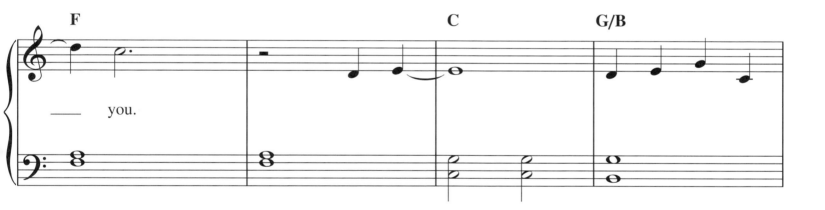

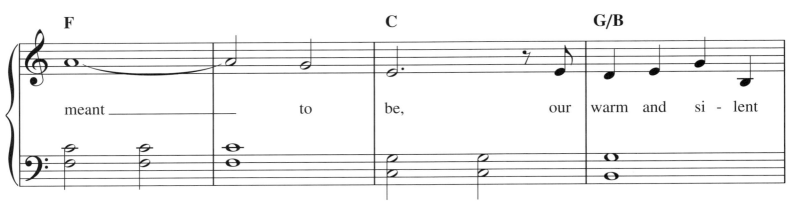

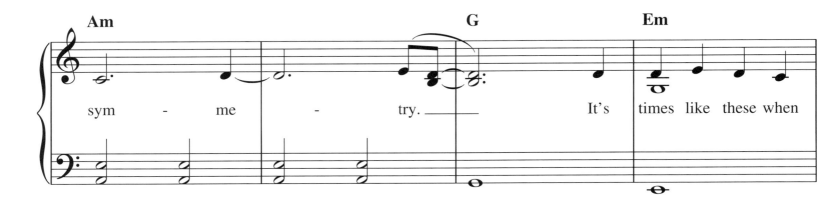

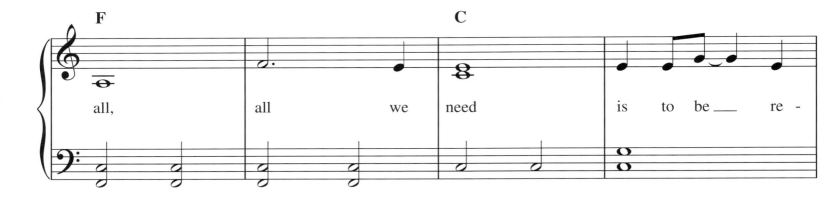

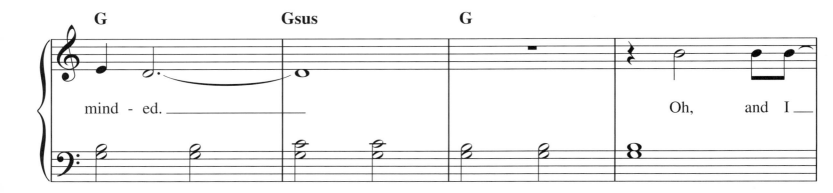

have flown _ a thou - sand miles _ to emp - ty rooms _ and

crowd - ed aisles. _ And we went from ca - the - dral bells to

show and tell __ and wish - you - wells. _ And I,

I still look at you, and I am blind -

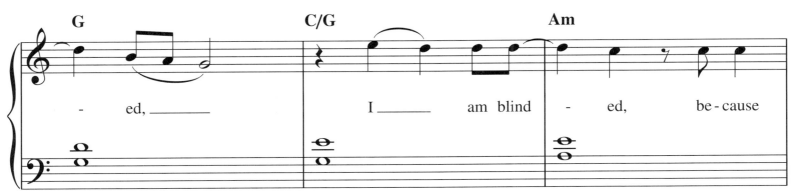

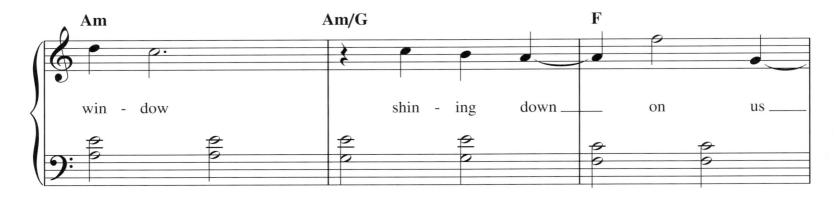

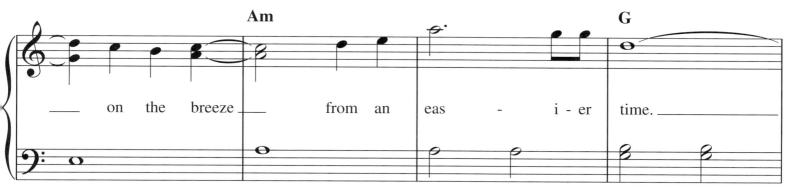

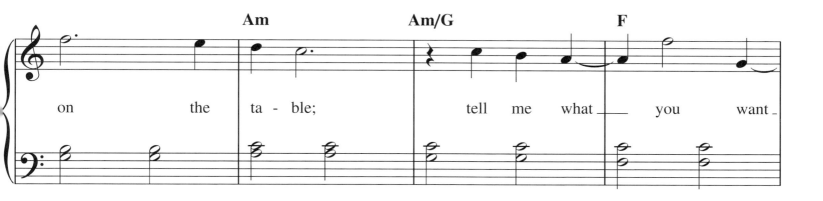

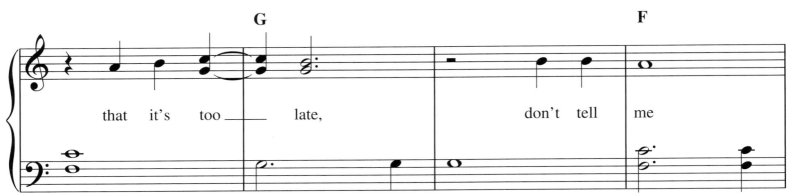

that   it's   too ____ late,   don't tell   me

that   it's   too ____ late ____ now, ____ just don't tell   me

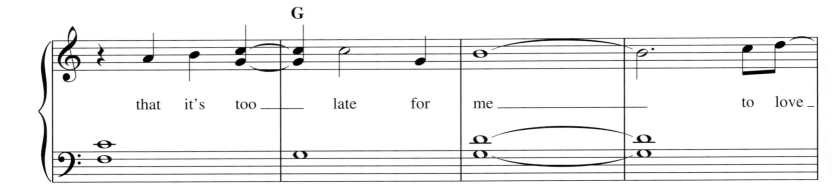

that   it's   too ____ late   for   me _____   to love _

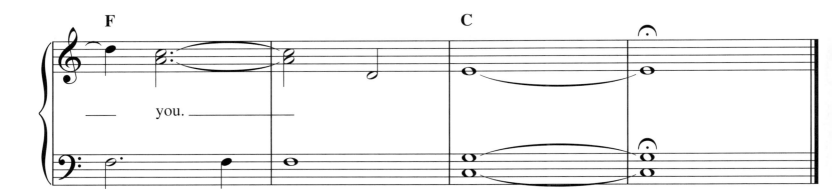

____ you. _____

IF I WALK AWAY

Words and Music by JOSH GROBAN
and DAN WILSON

Moderately, in one

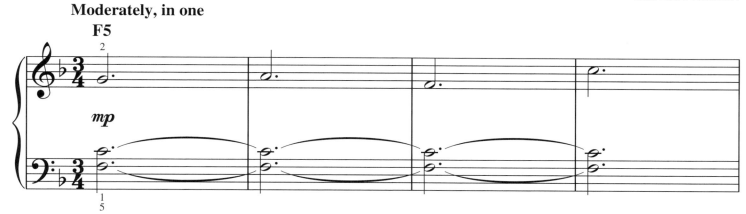

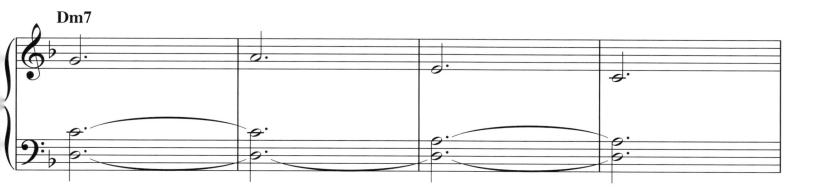

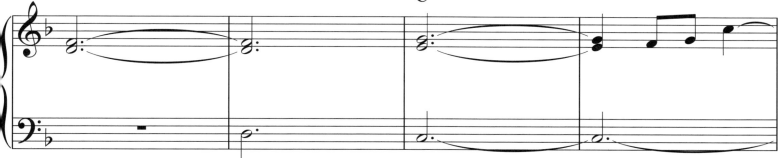

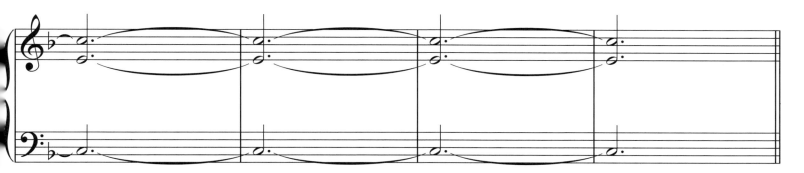

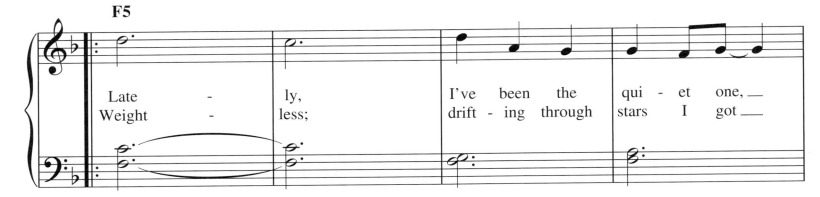

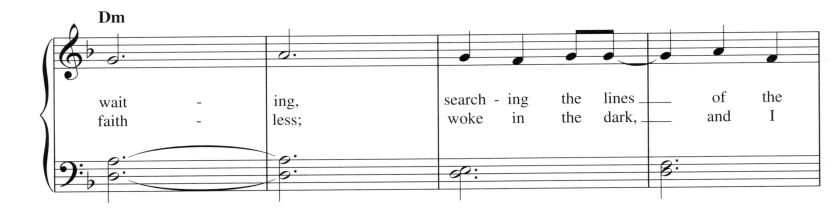

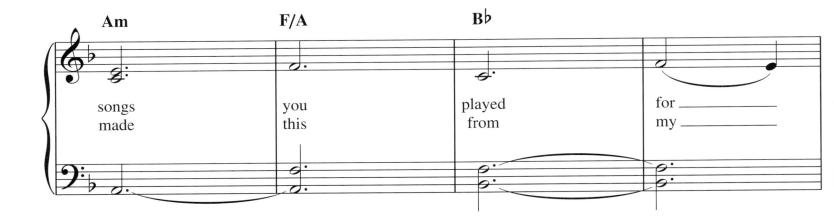

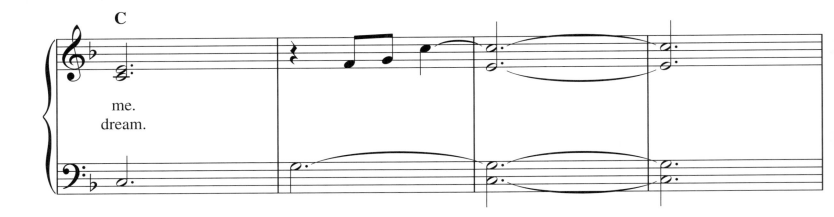

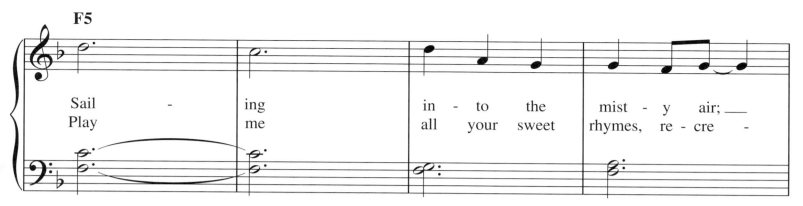

Sail - ing in - to the mist - y air;
Play me all your sweet rhymes, re - cre -

fad - ing, bound for I don't - know - where.
ate me. Now comes the time when I'll

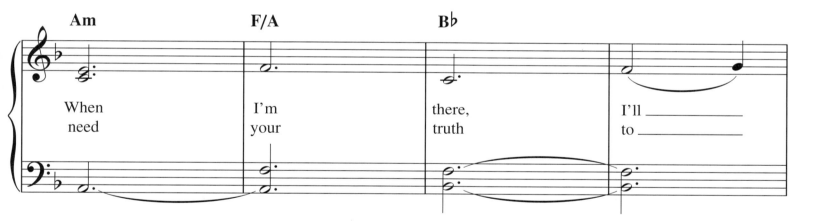

When I'm there, I'll
need your truth to

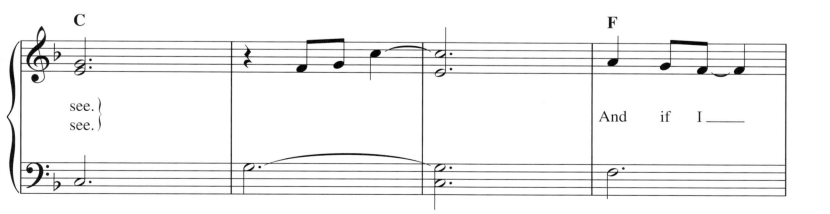

see.
see.

And if I

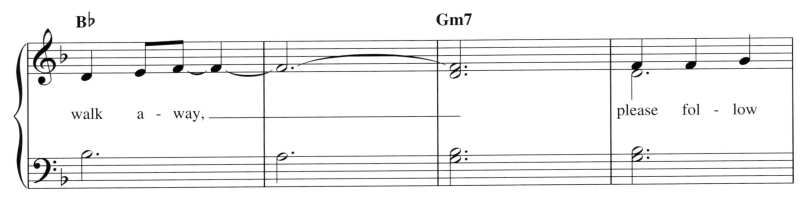

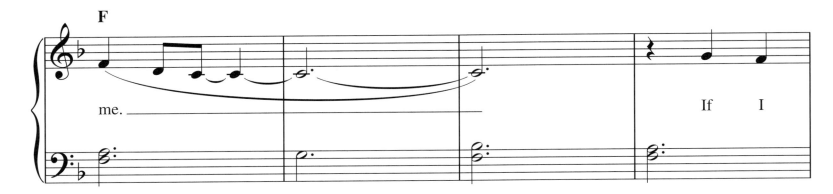

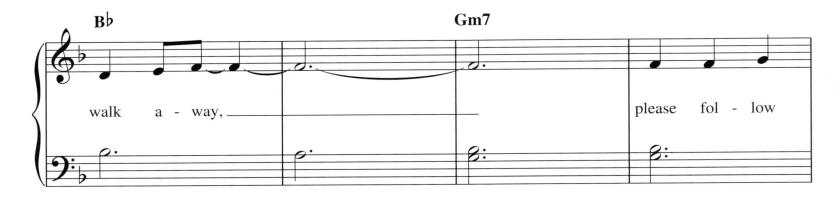

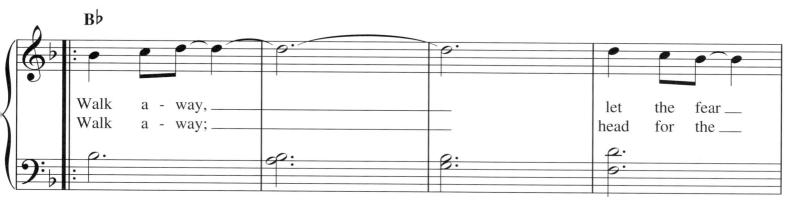

B♭

Walk a - way, _____ let the fear __
Walk a - way; _____ head for the __

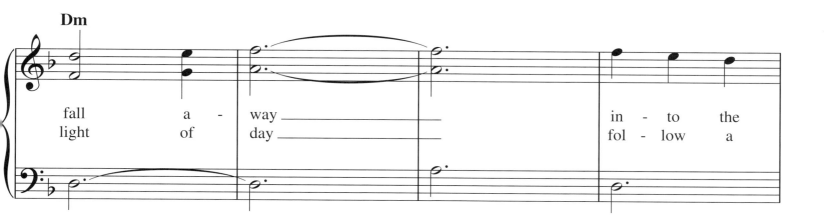

Dm

fall a - way _____ in - to the
light of day _____ fol - low a

C

fire you made, _____ scar - let and
bright - er way _____ out of the

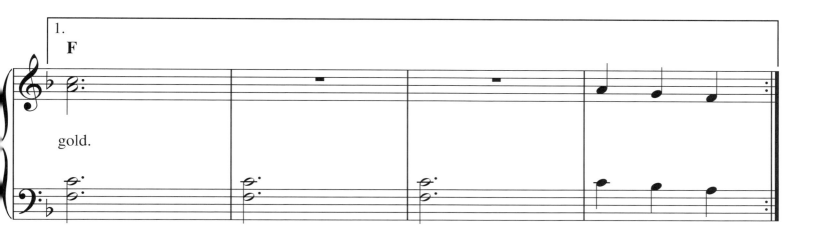

1.
F

gold.

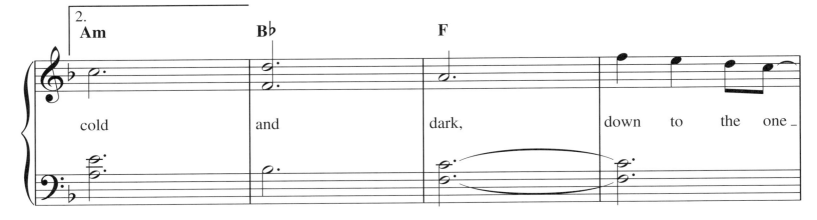

cold   and   dark,   down to the one_

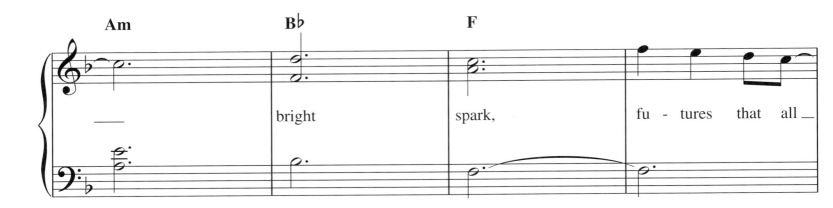

bright   spark,   fu - tures that all_

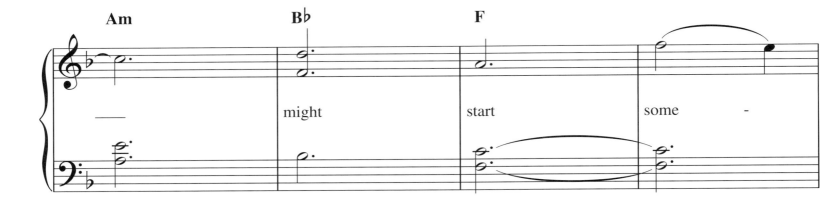

might   start   some -

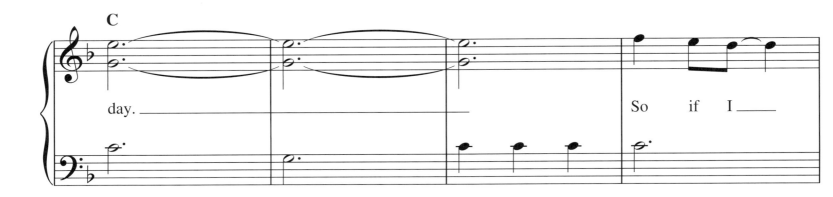

day. _____   So if I _____

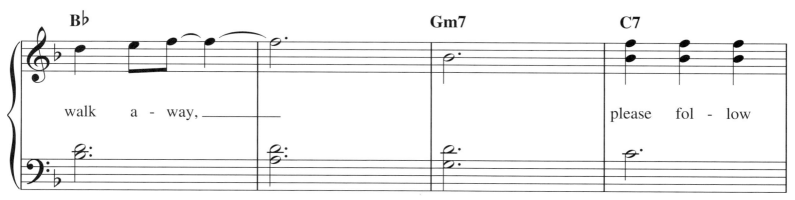

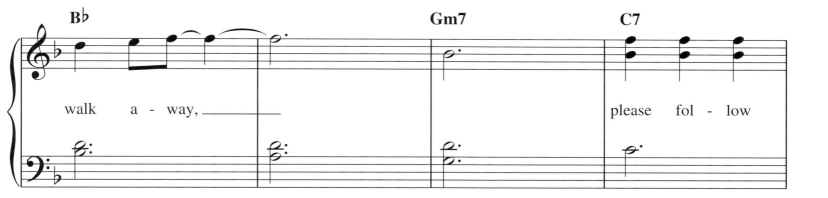

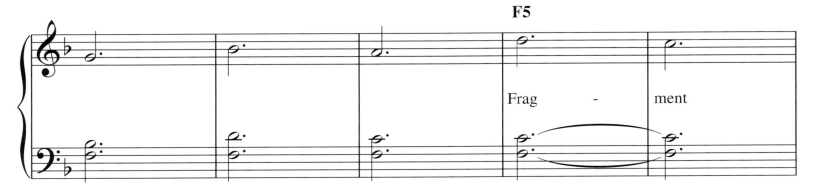

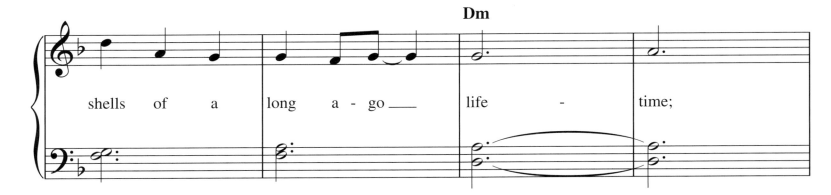

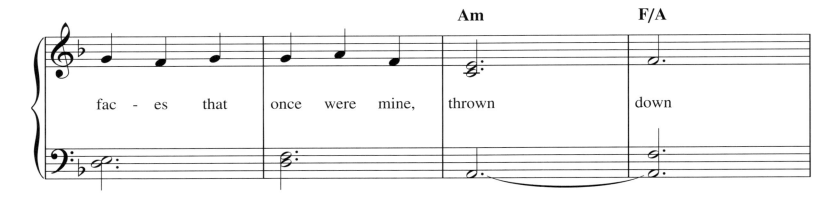

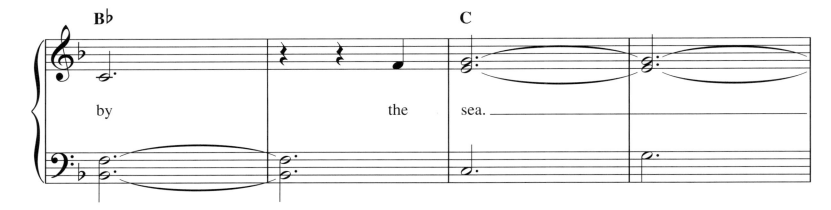

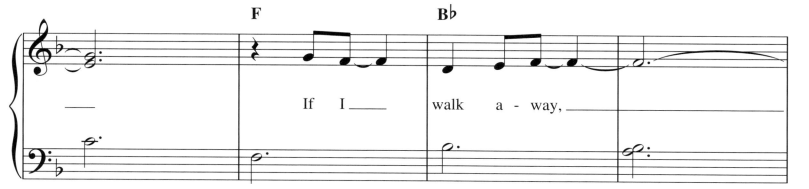

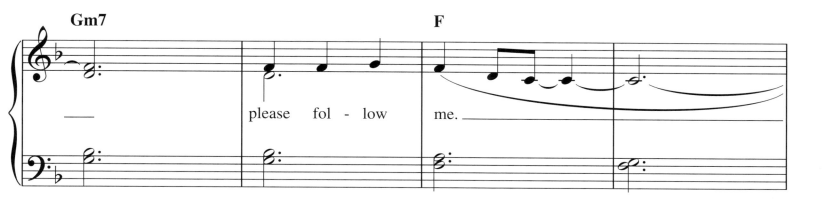

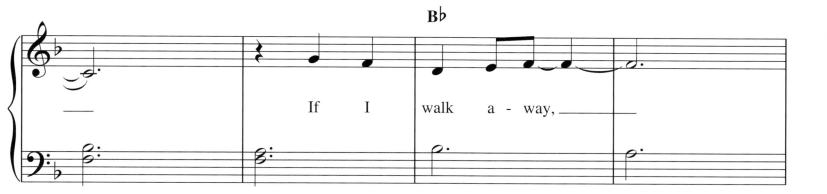

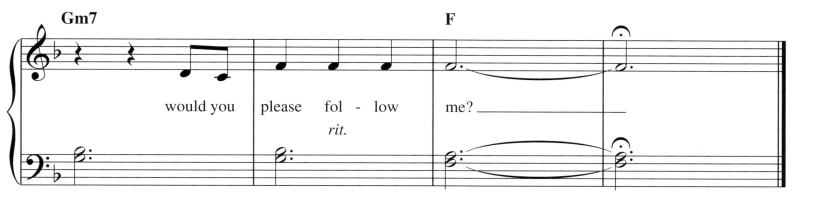

LOVE ONLY KNOWS

Words and Music by JOSH GROBAN
and DAN WILSON

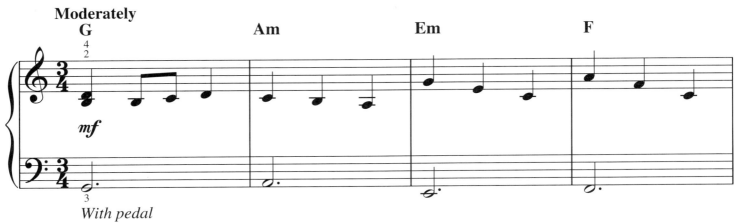

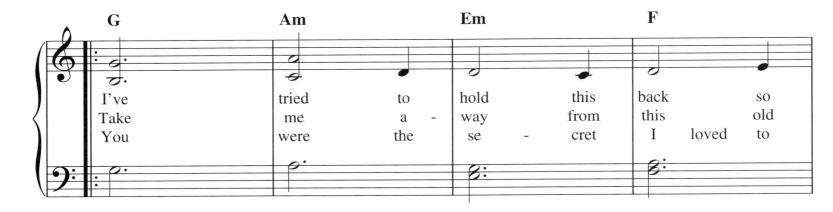

I've tried to hold this back so
Take me a - way this from this old
You were the se - cret I loved to

long. _____
game _____
keep, _____

And
of
the

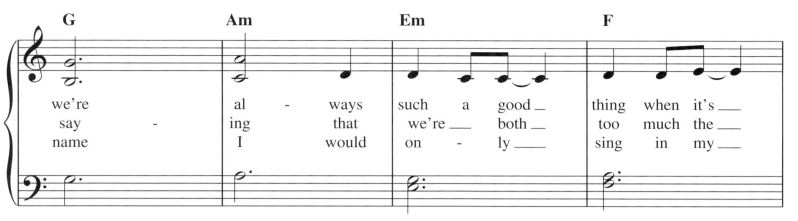

we're | al - ways | such a good __ | thing when it's __
say - | ing that | we're __ both __ | too much the __
name | I would | on - ly __ | sing in my __

gone. _____ | | Would it be al -
same. _____ | | Would it be al -
sleep. _____ | | Would it be al -

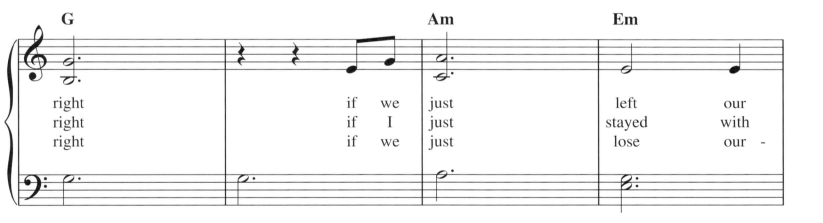

right | if we just | left our
right | if I just | stayed with
right | if we just | lose our -

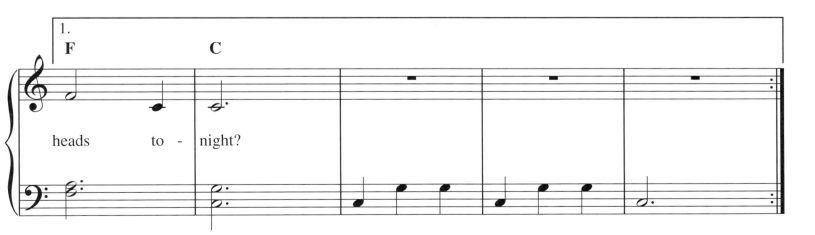

heads to - night?

you   to - night? _____   And
selves   to - night? _____   And

be - fore I   go;   will I ____   ev - er ____   see
if   you   let   go,   will you __   reach out __   a -

you a - gain? ____ ___   She said, "Love on - ly
gain? _____   She said, "Love on - ly

knows." _____   Love on - ly knows _
knows." _____

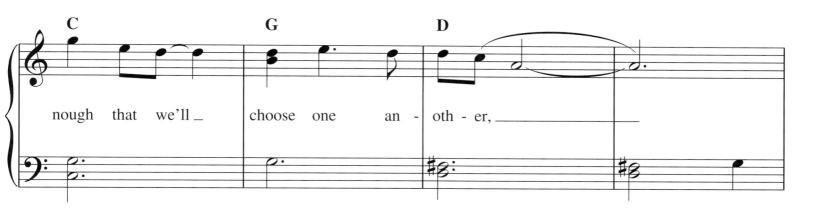

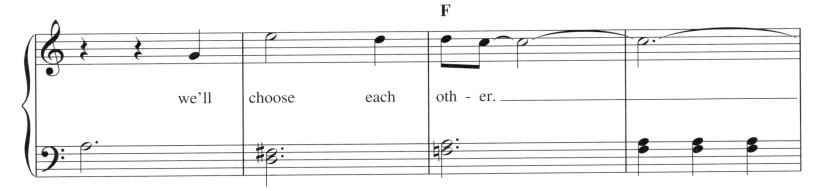

F

we'll   choose   each   oth - er. _____

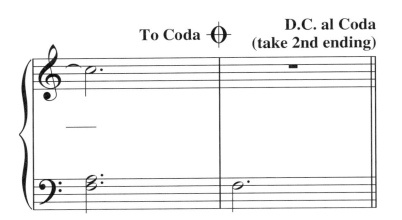

To Coda ⊕   **D.C. al Coda**
(take 2nd ending)

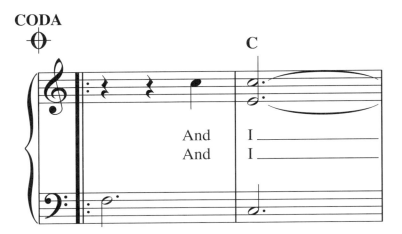

CODA ⊕   **C**

And   I _____
And   I _____

Em7/B   **Am7**

can't _____   breathe with - out _____
can't _____   live   with - out _____

G   **F**

you,   and   I _____   don't. _____
love,   and   I _____   won't, _____

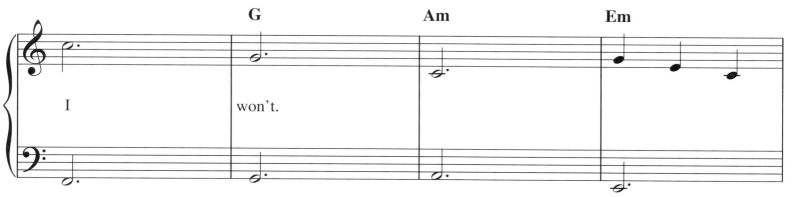

I   won't.

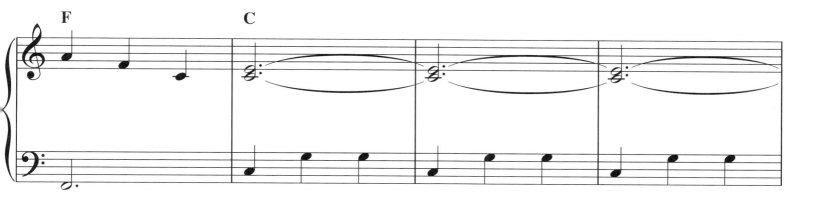

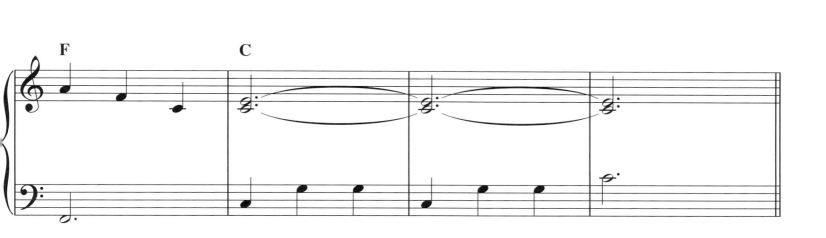

Love on - ly knows ___ if we'll give in to fear ___
Love on - ly knows ___ how your arms pull me in ___

___ and choose life un - der cov - er. ___
___ like the tide pulls me un - der. ___

She said, love on - ly knows ___ if it's
She said, love on - ly knows ___ just how

spe - cial e - nough that we'll ___ choose one an - oth - er. ___
long we can run be - fore ___ we lose each oth - er,

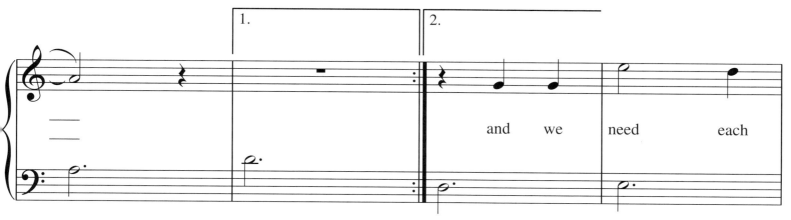

and we need each

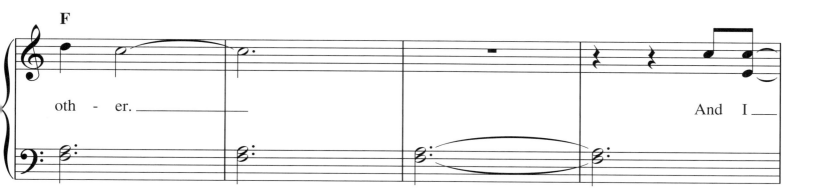

F

oth - er. And I

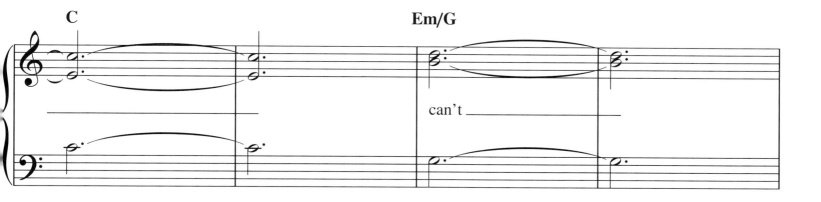

C   Em/G

can't

Am   G   F

live with - out you, and I won't.

VOCÊ EXISTE EM MIM

Words and Music by JOSH GROBAN,
LESTER MENDEZ and CARLINHOS BROWN

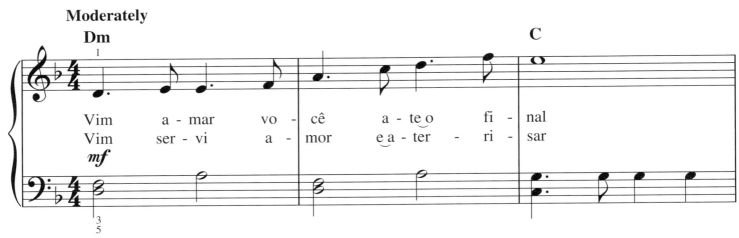

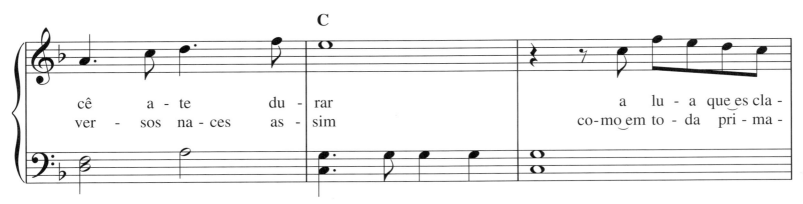

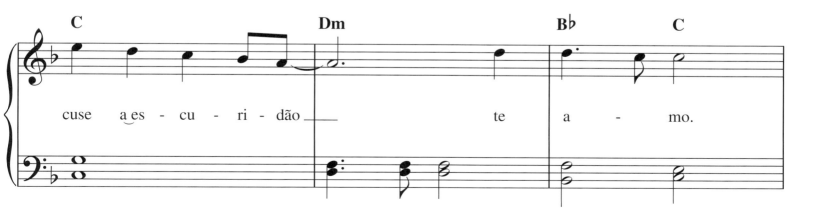

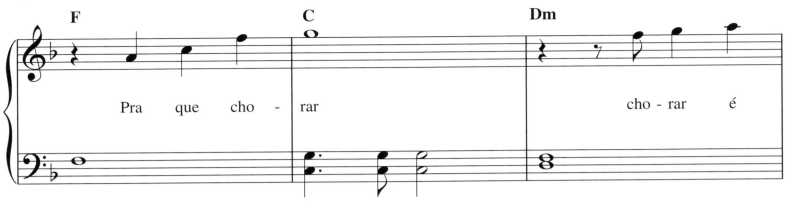

Pra que cho - rar   cho - rar é

To Coda

fim   vo - cê e - xi - ste em

1.

mim.

2. (♩ = ♩.)

mim.

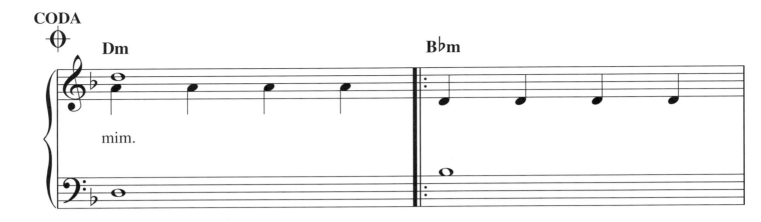

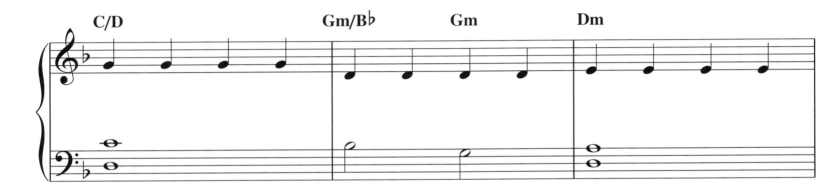

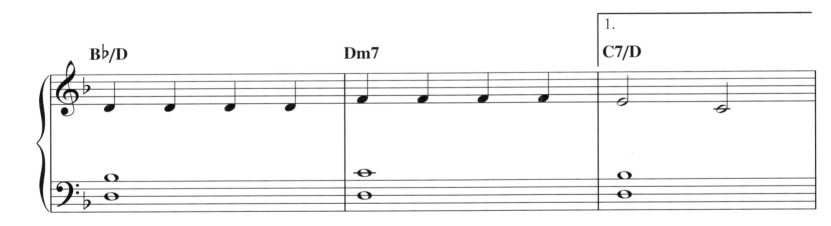

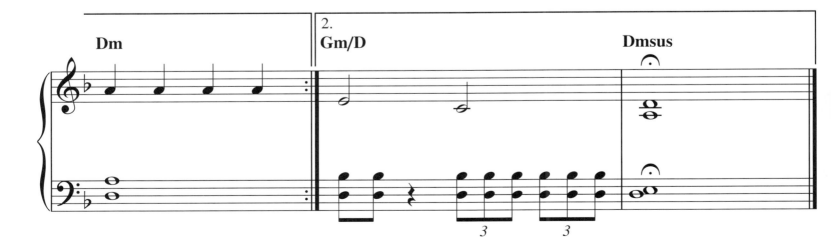

WAR AT HOME

Words and Music by JOSH GROBAN
and DAN WILSON

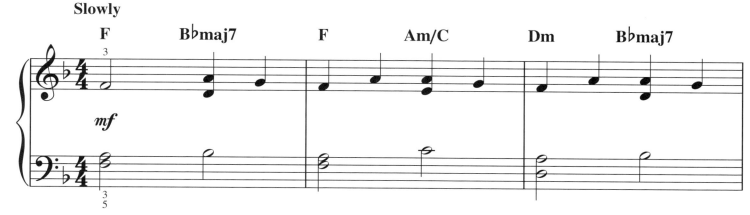

he just wants to run. And he's tired of be - ing told that he's the

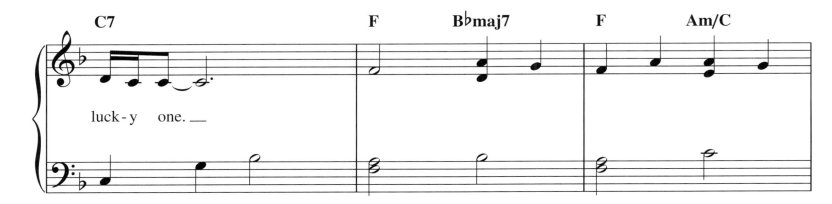

luck - y one.

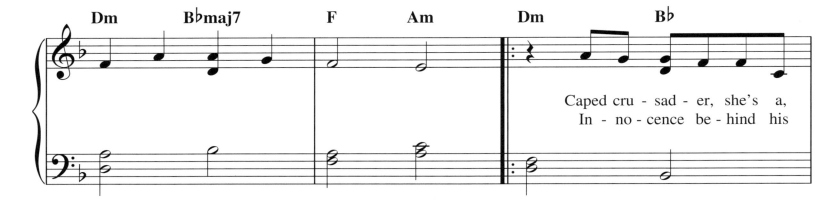

Caped cru - sad - er, she's a,
In - no - cence be - hind his

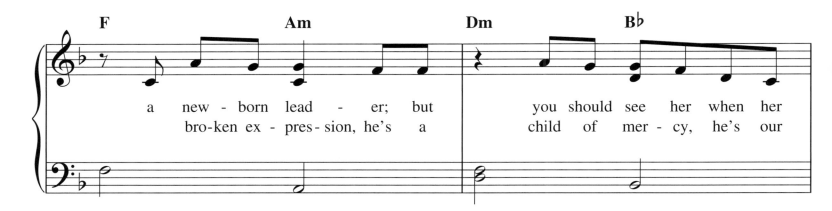

a new - born lead - er; but
bro - ken ex - pres - sion, he's a

you should see her when her
child of mer - cy, he's our

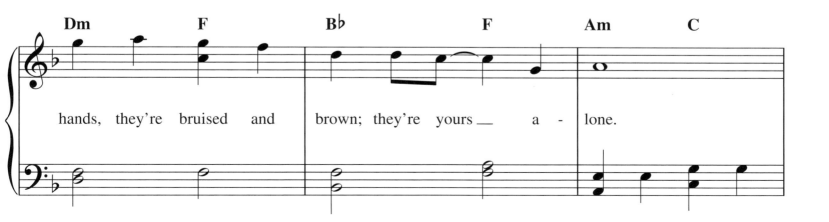

Hold on, ___ { love, now, } we're still go - ing down. Hold on, ___ { love, now, }

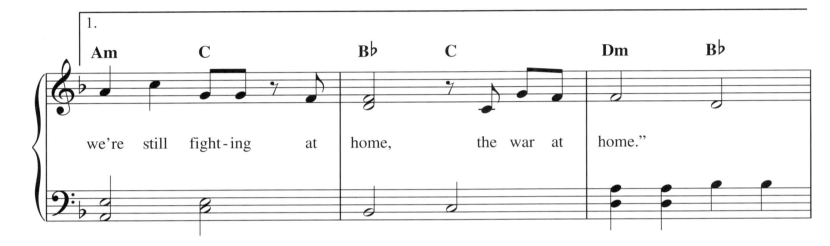

1.

we're still fight-ing at home, the war at home."

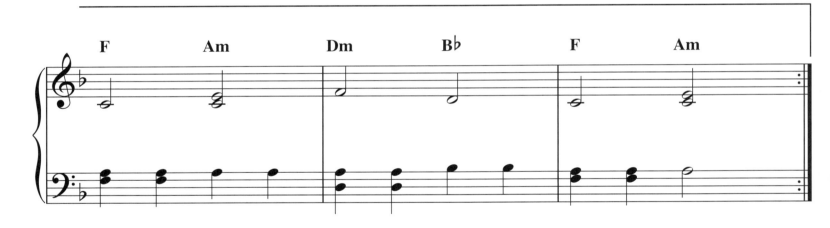

2.

we're still fight - ing, and it's..." (One step for - ward, two steps

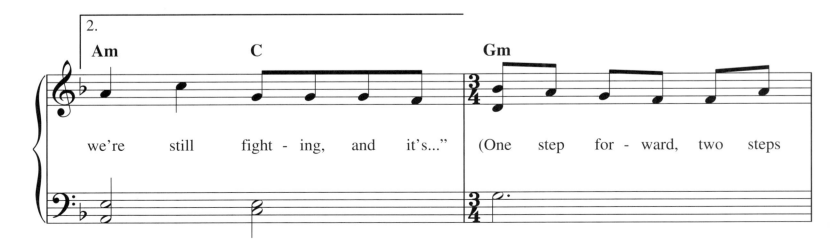

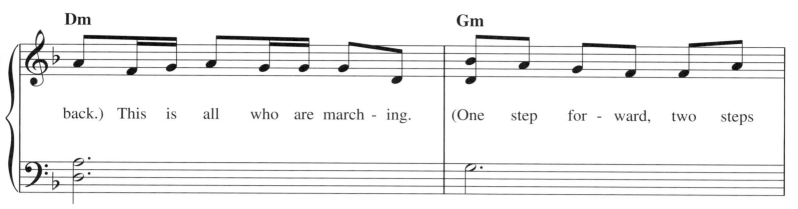

back.) This is all who are march - ing. (One step for - ward, two steps

back.) This is young at heart. (One step for - ward, two steps

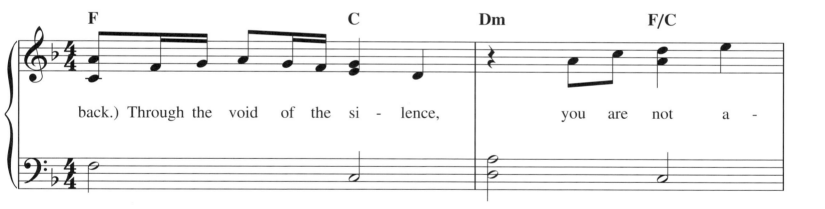

back.) Through the void of the si - lence, you are not a -

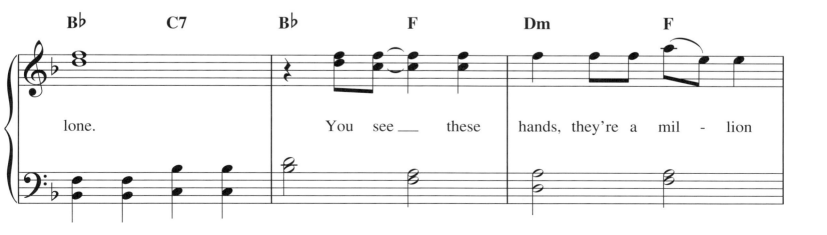

lone. You see ___ these hands, they're a mil - lion

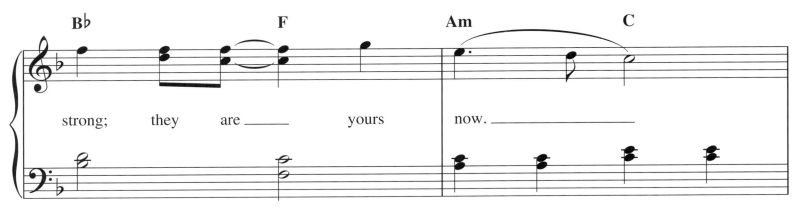

strong; they are _____ yours now. _____

Hold on, __ now, we're all __ go - ing down; hold on, __ now,

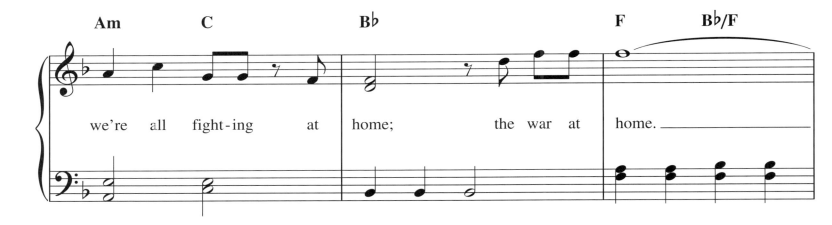

we're all fight-ing at home; the war at home. _____

_____ *rit.*

LONDON HYMN

Words and Music by JOSH GROBAN
and MARIUS DeVRIES

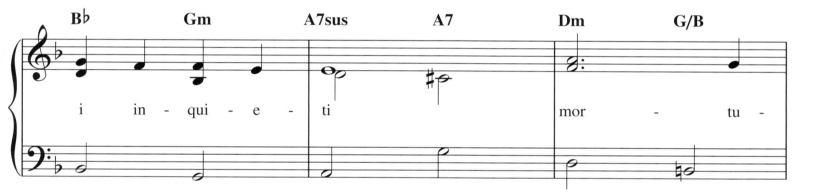

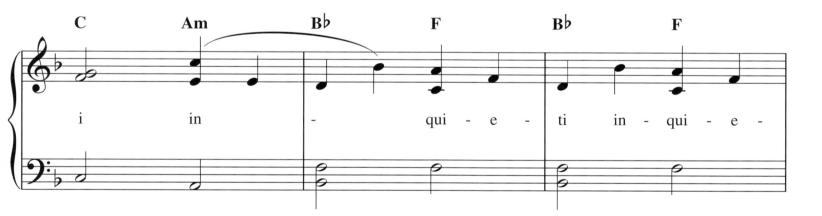

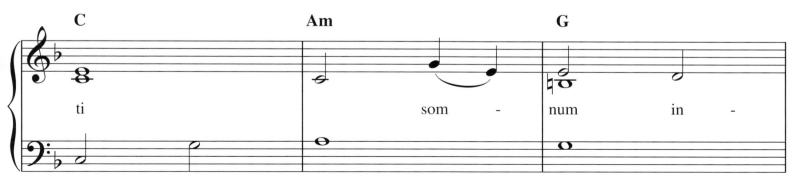

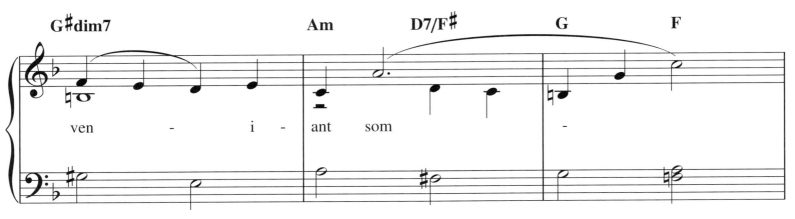

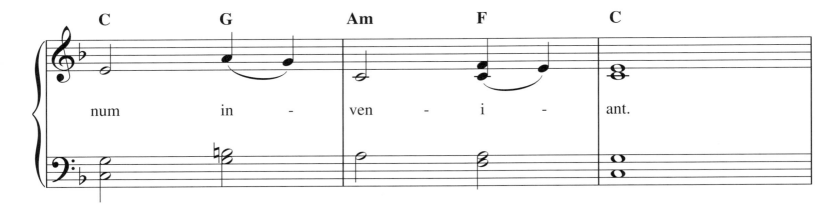

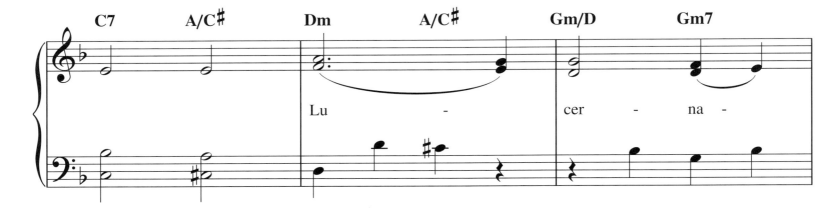

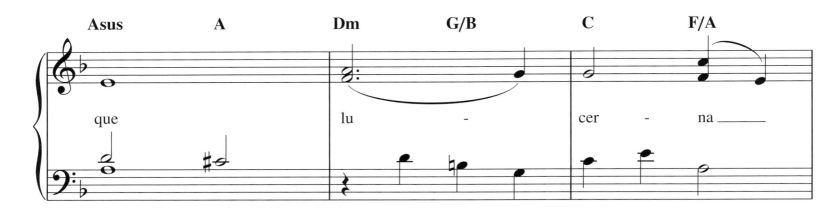

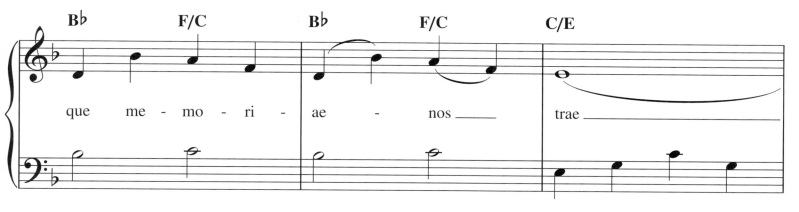

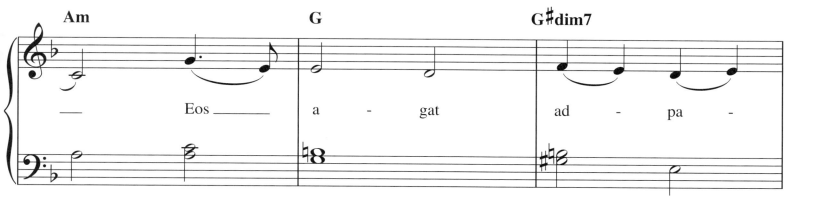

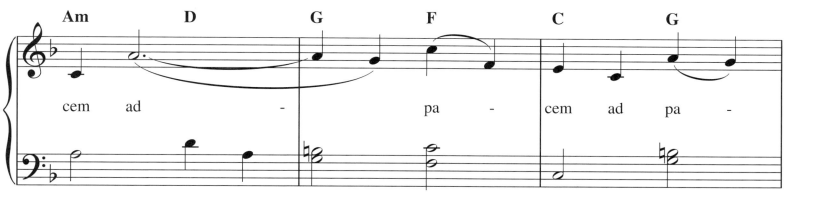

STRAIGHT TO YOU

Words and Music by
NICK CAVE

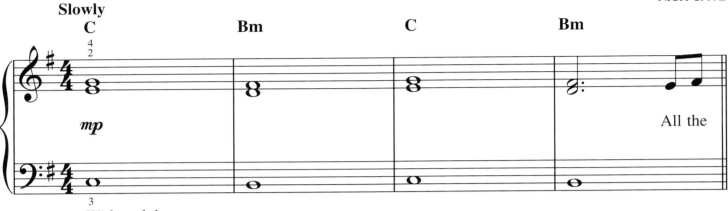

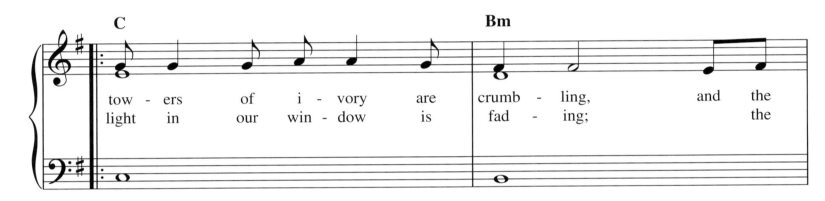

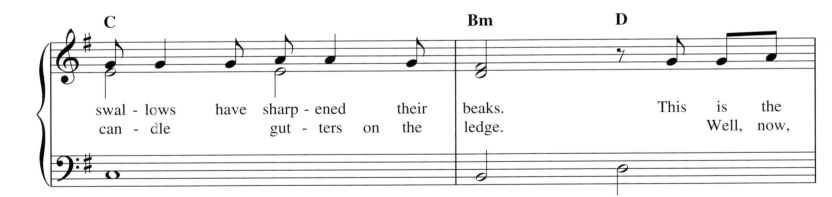

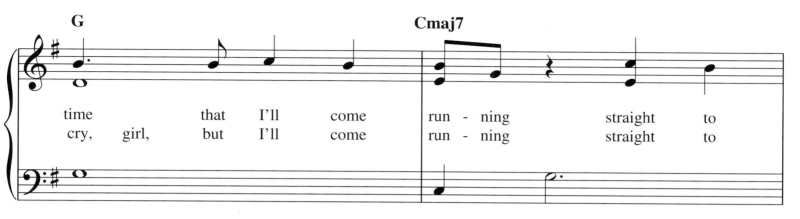

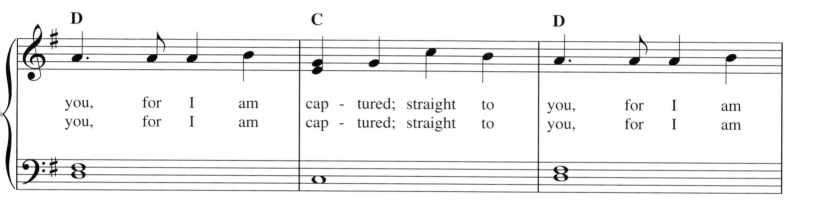

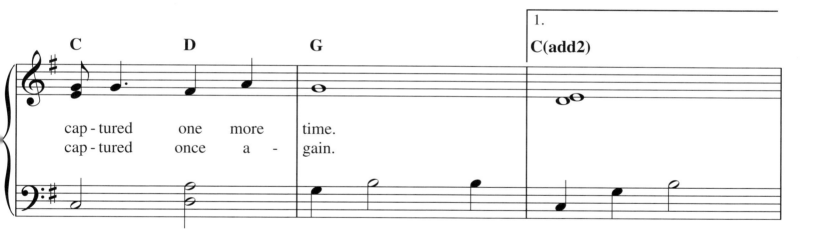

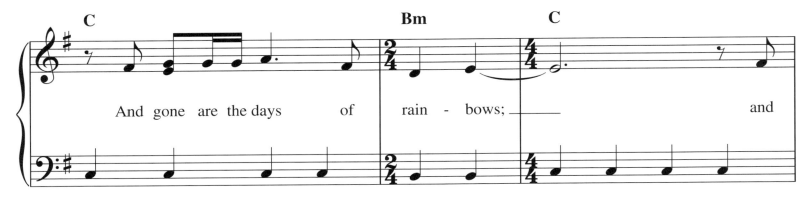

And gone are the days of rain - bows; _____ and

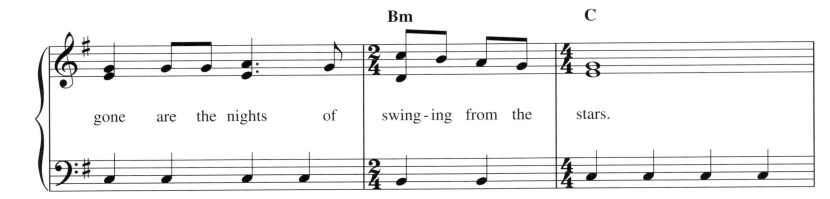

gone are the nights of swing-ing from the stars.

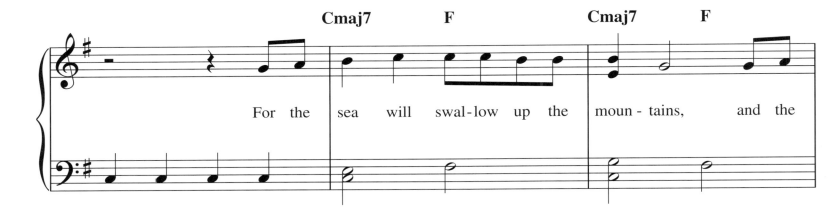

For the sea will swal-low up the moun - tains, and the

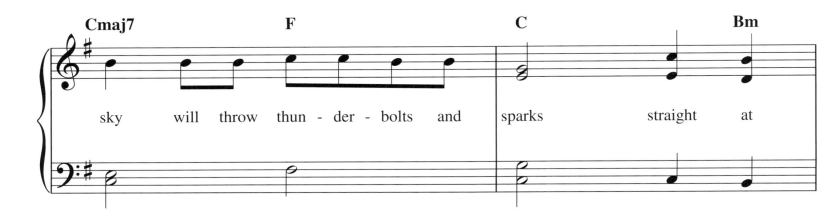

sky will throw thun - der - bolts and sparks straight at

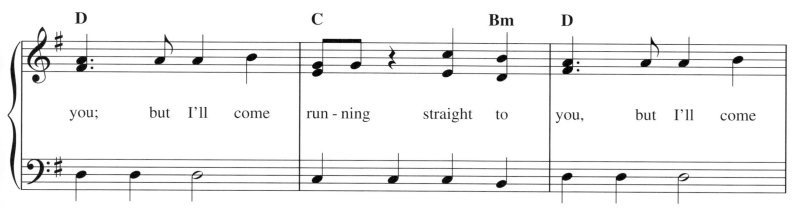

you; but I'll come run - ning straight to you, but I'll come

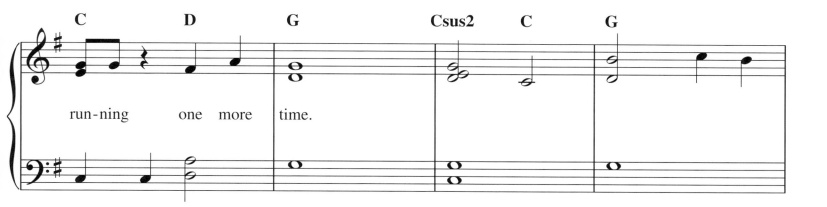

run-ning one more time.

Heav - en has de - nied us its king - dom; the

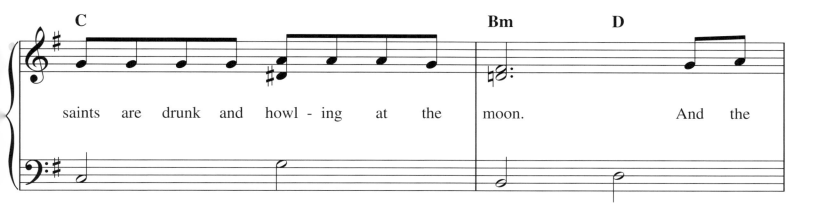

saints are drunk and howl - ing at the moon. And the

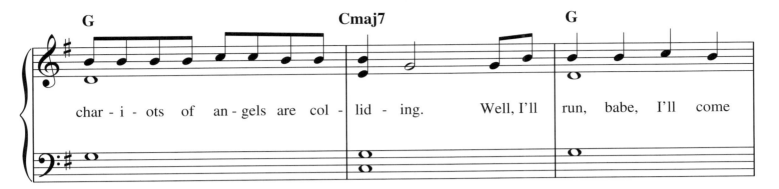

char - i - ots of an - gels are col - lid - ing. Well, I'll run, babe, I'll come

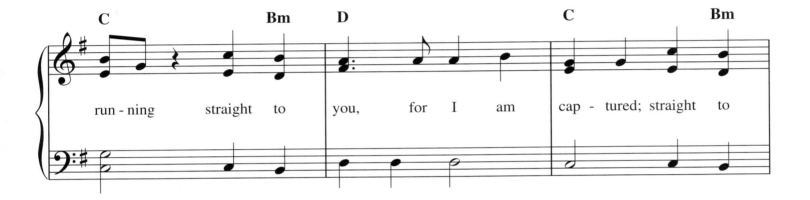

run - ning straight to you, for I am cap - tured; straight to

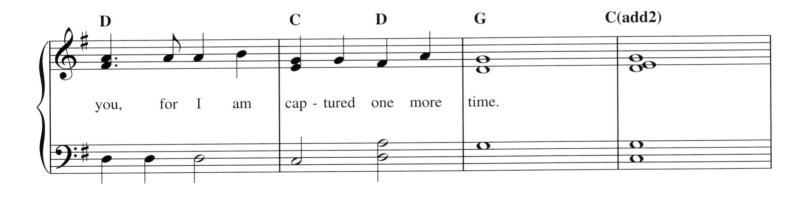

you, for I am cap - tured one more time.

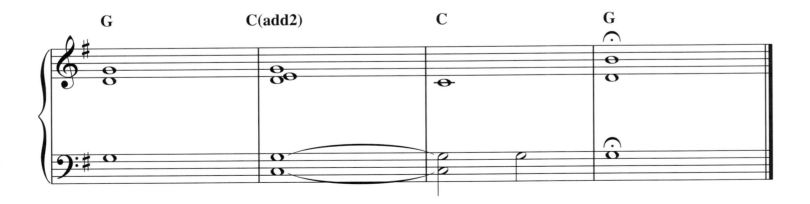